WALKING ON WHEELS

50 Wheel-friendly Trails in Scotland

Proceeds
from the sale of this book will go to
The WALKING ON WHEELS Trust

SC 036947

WALKING ON WHEELS

50 Wheel-friendly Trails in Scotland

Eva McCracken

Cualann Press

ISBN-10: 0-9544416-8-0
ISBN-13: 978-0-9544416-8-5

First Edition 2006

British Library Cataloguing in Publication Data. A catalogue record of this book is available at the British Library.

Printed by Polskabook

Published by Cualann Press Limited, 6 Corpach Drive, Dunfermline, KY12 7XG Scotland
Tel/Fax +44 (0)1383 733724
Email: info@cualann.com
Website: www.cualann.com

DEDICATION

Chris Davie

who inspired me to ramble on wheels in Fife and then all over Scotland

Chris Davie (1950-2005) believed in taking responsibility for his own actions and he was never one to sit at home. I only got to know Chris when he was in his late forties and had retired from the Fife Constabulary. Being in a wheelchair did not confine him; it liberated him. He used his battery-powered wheels to get out every day. His favourite haunt was Ravenscraig Park in Kirkcaldy, five minutes from his house. I'll never forget an audit of the park that we did together in 2000. At that time access to the shore path was challenging: definitely a red category path. Chris taught me never to go out alone or, if I did, always to tell someone where I was going and to take a fully charged phone with me.

Front Cover: A fine day at Loch Barnluasgan, near Bellanoch, Argyll.

Back Cover: Eva McCracken, the author, on a Beamer Tramper, Lady Mary's Walk, near Crieff.

CONTENTS

ACKNOWLEDGEMENTS

This book has been made possible with assistance from many individuals and organisations; some are mentioned below but there are others not named who will know of my gratitude.

I would first of all like to thank Mike Bruton, Chairman of Disabled Ramblers in England, who encouraged me in 1999 to set up a disabled rambling group in Scotland and who has supported me ever since; Ian Newman, Chief Executive Fieldfare Trust, who encouraged and supported the inaugural committee of Scottish Disabled Ramblers and who is still present at the end of the phone for me; Hugh Fife, Reforesting Scotland, who, from the beginning, has made helpful suggestions on where to ramble.

My unbounded gratitude goes to the following friends: Davy Campbell who had been rambling around Scotland for years before I even thought of doing so and who has been a constant source of help and advice; Margaret and Pete Sneddon who helped promote the idea of disabled rambling in Scotland; Jenny Haddow who in 2000 with her partner, Sandy, helped the Scottish Disabled Ramblers and more recently has become my social carer without whom my activities would be much curtailed.

I first encountered Countryside Rangers in 1999. They come from various backgrounds and although most have been to university they all seem ready and willing to work on a minimal wage, taking seasonal jobs before getting their feet under their desks. My thanks go to the many Countryside Rangers working all over Scotland who have accompanied me or advised me on nearly every trail.

To my husband, David, I give credit for sowing the seeds of this book of short wheel-friendly walks. Having seen a book on walks in Scotland which gave no indication of path surface, camber, gradient or barriers, he said, 'You could do that for wheelchair users.' I also thank him for his photographic skills and contributions, without which this book would be much duller. I am grateful for his tolerance and forbearance of my ever-increasing demands on his time to ferry me (and scooter) around Scotland and for his proof-reading skills.

Before setting out to write an information book on accessible trails in Scotland I successfully applied for a Level I Scotland UnLtd Seed Corn Award. Scotland UnLtd has supported me throughout. Ability Net and the Leonard Cheshire Workability Fund offered support and help in identifying and funding a computer with voice recognition and a keyboard and mouse suitable for my reduced dexterity. IT training was provided through my local college and by January 2005 I was ready to go.

My thanks most particularly go to my fellow board members on The Walking on Wheels Trust: Bob & Sue Walker; Gus & Heather Macdonald; Jim Latimer and David McCracken.

I am indebted to the following service providers whose assistance has been most helpful:

> Cairngorm National Park Authority
> Loch Lomond & The Trossachs National Park Authority
> British Waterways Scotland
> Ballater Royal Deeside Walking Week
> The Great Glen Way
> Lomond Hills Regional Park Partnership
> Pentland Hills Regional Park
> Water of Leith Conservation Trust

Without very generous sponsorship from the following, this book would not have been possible:

> Caledonian Challenge Courage Cup Winner (donation from Graham Leggatt)
> Paths to Health
> British Waterways Scotland
> Scottish Community Foundation (Sport Relief)
> Scotland UnLtd
> Forestry Commission Scotland
> Falkirk Council
> Ordnance Survey Maps (donation in kind)
> Fife Council
> Glenmore Lodge
> Family & friends

Finally, I would like to thank Roger Smith, guidebook writer and former editor of *TGO*, for many hours spent checking maps.

My thanks to all,
Eva McCracken

NOTE FOR THE READER

As someone who struggled to get around on walking sticks for a number of years before accepting that I needed to use a wheelchair, I now call my wheelchair my 'liberator'. The use of the wheelchair opened up whole areas of working and social life which had been closed to me because of the difficulty I had getting about. This book will go some way in further opening up the lives of people who rely on wheelchairs, permanently or temporarily, by providing a guide to where accessible walking routes exist. The enormous effort of planning a walk in the country should be a thing of the past.

I remember my only hill walk in a wheelchair. As the route was not adapted at all it required two very strong men and a wheelchair that never recovered. However, it was worth it for the sense of space and isolation I had never experienced before. For the first time I understood what my hill walking friends enjoyed in their leisure time. The walks in this book will, hopefully, not ruin your wheelchair but they will give you a taste of what it is like to be out and about in the countryside.

I hope you enjoy experiencing the walks in this book.

Anne Begg
MP for Aberdeen South

THE AUTHOR

Eva McCracken had been a keen walker before Multiple Sclerosis resulted in occasional and then more frequent use of a wheelchair. In 2000 she discovered the joys of exploring the outdoors using her electric wheelchair and her electric scooter. For the past five years she has collected information on trails accessible to wheelchair users in Scotland and has selected the top 50 routes, all with varying degrees of difficulty.

Eva practised as an Occupational Therapist north and south of the border in health and social care settings. Having lived with benign MS for twenty years she retired from clinical work in 1996. In 2000 she founded the Scottish Disabled Ramblers, which, since that time, has set up four regional groups in Scotland.

FOREWORD

The countryside belongs to all of us and as such we should all have access to it, provided we treat that right of access in a responsible manner. That's one of the fundamental tenets that I, and many others before me, have long lobbied and campaigned for.

Now, in the early years of the 21st century, there is a growing recognition that our countryside, the green world as opposed to the grey concrete world many of us live in, offers us a sanctuary, a haven, somewhere we can escape the growing pressures of burgeoning urbanisation.

For many – the climbers, the mountaineers, the Munro-baggers and the adventure racers – this green world is seen as an arena for challenge, to face risk and uncertainty, perhaps even to experience adventure, but there is no doubt that our countryside and wild landscapes offer us much more than just an adventure arena.

There is a discernible value in sitting quietly by the edge of a loch and watching a roe deer tip-toe down to the water's edge, or suddenly coming across a buzzard sitting on a telegraph pole, or enjoying the antics of a flock of chaffinches as they dart around your feet picking up the crumbs of your picnic sandwiches. There is a wonder in the changing of the seasons, as the harsh blandness of winter gives way to the new life of spring, and what could be finer than rambling through an autumn woodland as the flamboyant pageantry of nature makes one great final gesture before the inexorable cycle of nature takes us back into winter again.

The marvellous thing that Eva McCracken's book illustrates is that we can all witness such natural wonders; we can immerse ourselves in that natural world and be not only distant spectators but part of it all, as indeed we surely are. It's a phenomenon I like to refer to as 'wild land connection' when we suddenly realise we are not mere visitors to the natural world, but part of it, as surely as the roe deer, the buzzard or the chaffinches. And we can experience that connection by visiting wild landscapes on our own two legs, or in a wheelchair.

We are fortunate here in Scotland that we now have amongst the finest access legislation in Europe. That legislation also places a responsibility on local authorities to provide core path networks around our towns and cities. Many of these networks are already in place and many of the paths are wheelchair friendly. Eva has highlighted a number of routes to be enjoyed but the good news is that this huge network of paths is growing, allowing all of us to experience, and benefit from, the wonders of the green world.

I firmly believe we all have a small smouldering glow within us that harks back to those days before civilisation became divorced from the land. Often it just takes a small breeze from the green world to give flame to that glow and allow the fire to burn brightly within us. My hope is that this book will provide that breeze for many, fanning the flames of wild land love and appreciation for those who may have thought a living relationship with the green world was beyond them.

Cameron McNeish
President, Ramblers Scotland

INTRODUCTION

To describe disabled rambling I would like to quote my friend, James Page, who was the Press Officer for Scottish Disabled Ramblers from 2000 to 2003. The organisation was disbanded in 2004.

> Scottish Disabled Ramblers is a random selection of people with two things in common – some form of disability and a love of the countryside. Whatever barriers the first of these might appear to put in the way of the second can be overcome. Major obstacles might seem to be logistical ones of equipment and finance, but with enough commitment and energy such obstacles can be minimised … What could be better on a mild Saturday in January than a good brisk walk in the countryside? Agreed, and compared with the excess of the festive season and the lethargy of the TV-soap generation it's both physically and morally sound.

These are the words of a man who said of himself that he could fall off a gangplank the width of the M8. I hope the publication of this book will encourage everybody to do as he did and to get back out there and enjoy the fresh air and countryside.

The walks I have chosen for this book have all been visited by me in my scooter or electric wheelchair over a period of five years. Where possible the information has been checked to take account of recent developments. As the work of many service providers to improve access is ongoing, some recent changes might not be recorded. Furthermore, some minor changes due to natural erosion or growth of vegetation could have taken place.

I have restricted my choice to 2–12 mile trails (3–19 km) with various levels of difficulty. The paths through the Local Authority parks are on the whole easier, either because they are better surfaced or because parking and toilets are more likely to be available. For the more adventurous I have sought out longer, usually linear, paths which I have accessed in my electric wheelchair or scooter and which offer a good day out in more open countryside. My grading system is subjective but I hope as you try out the trails you will get to know it and find it useful.

Having a vehicle that suits the trail is important. I have found the Beamer Tramper (see photo on back cover) excellent, especially on difficult terrain. A new improved model is expected in 2006. The better the vehicle, the more trails are accessible for the disabled.

Recent legislation is helping to further disabled rambling in Scotland. Many elements of the Disability Discrimination Act 1995 had been implemented by 2004 and the Land Reform (Scotland) Act 2003 became a reality. As a result of the Land Reform Act, the Scottish Outdoor Access Code was drawn up by Scottish Natural Heritage (SNH). The code provides guidance on the responsibilities of those taking recreation as well as those managing the land. Before setting off on a trip it is very important to 'know the Code before you go …' You will find a short version of the Code printed inside the back cover of this book. A full version can be obtained from SNH offices.

All Access Authorities (32 Local Authorities and the 2 National Parks) have been charged with establishing a Local Access Forum for their area to advise them on the delivery of their duties under the Land Reform Scotland Act. Most Scottish Local Authorities now employ an Access Officer who works alongside the Local Access Forum. To confuse matters, there are Access Officers also working alongside Disability Access Forums, usually composed of disabled people, to give advice on all access issues. It is important to be aware that should you feel discriminated against when trying to access the Scottish countryside, you now have two recent Acts and two local Forums to help you.

So, we have legislation recognising the rights of everyone, and an Access Code to guide us. The trails are being improved and our weather is generally not too harsh. My hope now is that readers will be encouraged to venture into our wonderful countryside.

For information on Access matters or for contact details for Access staff in Scotland not provided in the book please visit www.pathsforall.org.uk

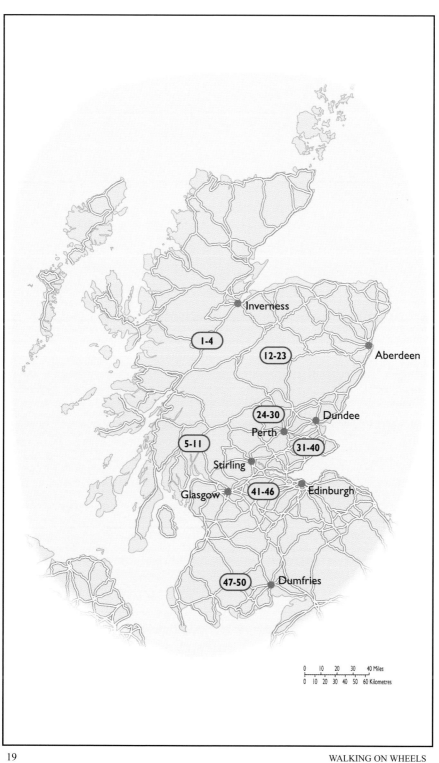

Inverness

1-4

12-23

Aberdeen

24-30

Dundee

Perth

5-11

31-40

Stirling

Glasgow

41-46

Edinburgh

47-50

Dumfries

| 0 | 10 | 20 | 30 | 40 Miles |
| 0 | 10 | 20 | 30 | 40 | 50 | 60 Kilometres |

THE GREAT GLEN

The Great Glen follows an impressive glacial fault running south-west to north-east across Scotland. The Glen is characterised by dramatic and beautiful scenery including Lochs Lochy, Oich and of course Loch Ness, one of the most famous stretches of water in Scotland. The lochs are linked by the Caledonian Canal.

The Caledonian Canal is a fantastic feat of engineering masterminded by the great Thomas Telford. It took over twenty years to complete and cut out the need for a very dangerous sea passage through the Pentland Firth. The canal was opened in 1822 and there are 29 locks along its length.

The Great Glen Way path, which runs up the Glen from Fort William to Inverness, is 73 miles (116 km) long and is the youngest of the Scottish family of long distance routes. The Way was opened in April 2002.

Over 80% of the Great Glen Way is now achievable for motorised buggies, and many of the paths and tracks can be accessed for day trips and wildlife encounters. This section of the book offers a variety of walks and routes for people with reduced mobility to try the Great Glen in bite-sized chunks. Come and experience the Highlands from the towpaths, forest tracks and drove roads, or join us for a ranger-led walk.

The Great Glen Way Rangers offer help and advice and an events programme each year. This can be found on www.greatglenway.com along with interesting information on the area, where to stay and eat and what else you can do. The Great Glen Way route manager is on 01320 366633.

For general enquiries about outdoor access or for reporting access issues in the Great Glen area, please contact the Outdoor Access Officer – Inverness end on 01463 702186 and Fort William end on 01397 707050.

The Great Glen

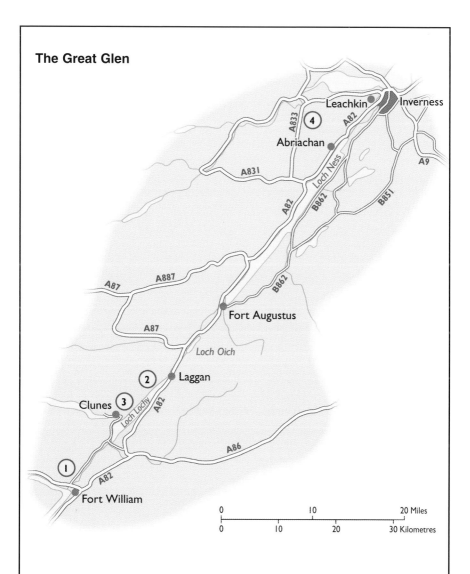

Trail Number	Name	Distance (Miles/Km)
1	Fort William to Clunes	12/19
2	Clunes to Laggan	8/13
3	Clunes, Mile Dorcha	3/5
4	Abriachan to Inverness	6/10

1 Fort William to Clunes

The Great Glen Way begins in Fort William near the car park at Morrisons. The supermarket is easily found close to the town centre.

This is not a very beautiful beginning to a very beautiful trail. I recommend that you miss out Fort William and begin from Neptune's Staircase near Banavie. There is a mild gradient at Neptune's Staircase but the surface of the towpath is stable and flat. However, I have designated it a yellow path because of distance and occasional potholes.

The towpath from here to Gairlochy is 6 miles. Enjoy the rural walk with a fine variety of trees and good views of the mountains. These include Britain's highest peak, Ben Nevis (1344 m), which is a magnet for climbers and is snow-capped for much of the year.

At Gairlochy the canal goes under the A8004, and at this point the Great Glen Way veers away from the canal, over the bridge and then right towards Clunes on to the A8005. You may wish to follow the trail on this road or park approximately ½ mile further on where the trail takes a sharp right down a very steep (1:5), but short, gradient towards Loch Lochy. The trail continues on a rough path near the edge of Loch Lochy where the little rivers running into the loch that once were forded are now crossed by bridges. After 1½ miles the trail comes back on to the road for a further mile to the Forest Walk at Clunes where there is parking.

Although this stretch of the GGW is not the most spectacular, it is well worth a visit. Note that this is a linear walk; you will either have to return the same way or arrange to be collected at Clunes.

FURTHER INFORMATION

Great Glen Way: 01320 366633 www.greatglenway.com
British Waterways Highland Canals' Customer Service Manager: 01463 725500
Access Officer (Lochaber): 01397 707050

FACT FILE

Map	Ordnance Survey Landranger Sheet 41
Start	Fort William (NN 103742)
Finish	Clunes (NN 205886)
Parking	Fort William, Gairlochy & Clunes
Toilets	Morrisons W/C (L); BW Banavie W/C (L&R). Key-purchase through https://www.chandleryshop.com
Distance	11 miles / 18 km one way
Landscape	Waterscape / mountains / forest / waterfall

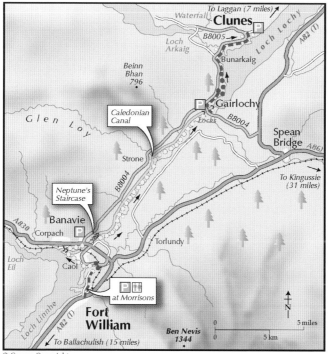

Neptune's Staircase (courtesy of Colin Simpson)

2 Clunes to Laggan

Great Glen Way (GGW)

Start at Clunes where there is plenty of space to leave your car. The yellow route from Clunes is a forest track all the way. As this is a working forest, the paths are occasionally diverted, but these diversions may not always be accessible to wheels. It is well worth phoning either the Great Glen Way or the Forestry Commission to check before you set off. Be aware also that most of the section is shared with the Cycle Route, but I have never found cyclists to be anything but pleasant and helpful.

Although this is a long path with few natural breaks, it offers stunning views of Loch Lochy. There are mountains all around and on a good day, with high blue skies, you can experience the spectacular. When you reach the cemetery at Kilfinnan with a large mausoleum for Glengarry chiefs, the track becomes a minor road which you could continue along to Laggan where on-road parking is possible. Or if you want a challenge, continue on the Great Glen Way which goes off to the right, through a chalet park and down to Laggan Locks. The pedestrian access crossing the lock is wide enough for most scooters but has a high step which requires a small ramp or a very strong helper. From here the GGW is narrow and fairly difficult for wheelchairs until you reach the A82. This is a very busy road, but the cars are periodically stopped for canal traffic at Laggan Bridge. A mile further on, the Great Glen Water Park has a coffee shop, restaurant, toilets and chalet accommodation.

For both my visits to the GGW I was fortunate in having the GGW Ranger with me. There were a few gates along the forest tracks, but I hope that on your visit to the GGW these barriers will have been removed.

FURTHER INFORMATION

Great Glen Way: 01320 366633 www.greatglenway.com
British Waterways Highland Canals' Customer Service Manager: 01463 725500
Access Officer (Lochaber): 01397 707050
Lochaber Forestry Commission 01397 702184

FACT FILE	
Map	Ordnance Survey Landranger Sheet 34
Start	Clunes (NN 203886)
Finish	Laggan (NN 304984)
Parking	Clunes, Laggan & GGWater Park
Toilets	GGWater Park café W/C (R)
Distance	8 miles / 13 km one way
Landscape	Waterscape / mountains / forest

WALKING ON WHEELS

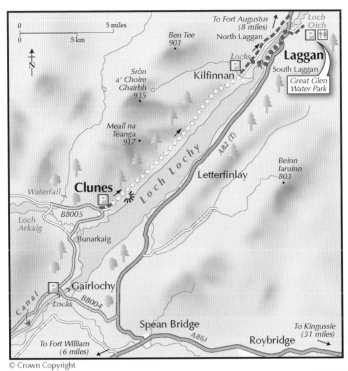

© Crown Copyright

Braving the elements along Loch Lochy

3 Clunes: Mìle Dorcha

Great Glen Way (GGW)

If you are looking for a shorter walk, suitable by wheelchair, then I would suggest a circular walk from the Forest Walk car park at Clunes. Head back west towards the B8005 and follow it through Mìle Dorcha (the Dark Mile). This is a mysterious, gloomy stretch of road which warrants its name and is dark in all seasons. As the valley widens you will see a magnificent waterfall which is the waters of the Allt Cia-aig falling into the Witch's Cauldron (see photograph). Continue over the hump-backed bridge, then turn left on to land owned by the Camerons of Lochiel. Continue along the estate road which takes you past the eastern end of Loch Arkaig. Turn left and you'll soon reach the Clan Cameron Museum. It is open in the afternoon daily from April to October and covers the history of the clan and its Jacobite links.

Although this trail is not part of the official Great Glen Way, it is mentioned in Jacquetta Megarry's book by Rucksack Readers called *The Great Glen Way*. This is an ideal companion for my first four walks.

The estate, like many estates in Scotland, has a marvellous selection of trees from around the world. In the 18th & 19th centuries, many of the Scottish landed gentry imported small seedlings from their travels. It also became a tradition to try to emulate the English estate owners by planting Copper Beech trees to mark a particular site of interest, for instance, a church. Try spotting a Copper Beech tree and make your guess as to what might have been once situated nearby in sight of the house.

Continue through the estate to return to the B8005 and back around to the car park at Clunes.

FURTHER INFORMATION

Great Glen Way: 01320 366633 www.greatglenway.com
Access Officer (Lochaber): 01397 707050

FACT FILE

Map	Ordnance Survey Landranger Sheet 34
Start and Finish	Clunes (NN 203886)
Parking	Clunes
Toilets	Clan Cameron Museum, outside, walk in; GGWater Park café W/C (R)
Distance	3 miles / 5 km circular
Landscape	Dark, ancient forest & magnificent waterfall

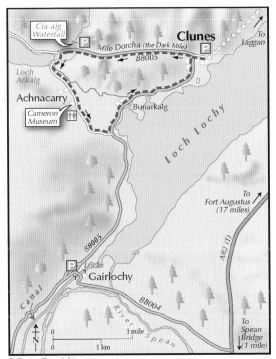

Ferocious waterfall after heavy rain

4 Abriachan to Inverness

Much of the Great Glen Way between Fort Augustus and Drumnadrochit is impassable by wheelchair. For a walk to Inverness I set off from Abriachan. Drive north from Drumnadrochit on the A82 for about 4 miles, then turn sharp left on a hairpin bend where you are advised to wait on the right-hand side until the road is clear. One mile later you will reach Abriachan. Fork left and a mile further on turn left again where the GGW crosses the road. This forest track will take you to the car park for 'Abriachan Community Woodland, the Highland Access Network', managed by the Abriachan Forest Trust which advertises over 9 miles of easy access paths suitable for wheelchairs and buggies. I visited in 2004 with Mike Bruton, Chair of Disabled Ramblers from Surrey, along with his wife and my husband. We took the wooden walkway and visited the fully scooter-accessible bird hide overlooking Loch Laide.

From there we all followed the GGW to the other minor road north from Abriachan and then I went on my own with a head full of numbers to and through the Aird Estate from Blackfold. A head full of numbers? This was the combination to open the padlocked gates – available from GGW Rangers. Having a sieve of a memory I wrote it down and set off with arrangements to meet the other three at Leachkin, to the west of Inverness. It was a wonderful experience, travelling occasionally at 6 mph through a dank, atmospheric forest and creating my own fantasies en route.

With the reassurance of mobile phone connection I didn't feel at risk and we were able to meet up half a mile from Leachkin at a small reservoir. This proved to be 'sensible' as the descent was challenging because of the gradient.

FURTHER INFORMATION

Great Glen Way: 01320 366633 www.greatglenway.com
Access Officer (Inverness & Nairn) 01463 702186

FACT FILE

Map	Ordnance Survey Landranger Sheet 26
Start	Abriachan (NH 541354)
Finish	Leachkin (NH 636448)
Parking	Abriachan Community Woodland; on road at Blackfold; P at Leachkin
Toilets	Abriachan Community Woodland W/C (L)
Distance	8 miles / 13 km one way
Landscape	Moorland and forest with accessible bird hide

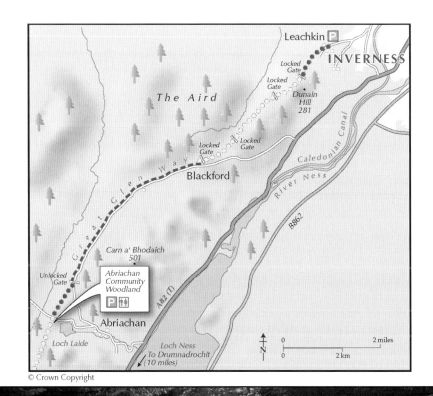

Walkway to bird hide

ARGYLL, LOCH LOMOND & THE TROSSACHS

Argyll and Bute Council covers the second largest geographical area of any Scottish local authority, stretching for over 100 miles from Appin in the north to Campbeltown in the south, and more than 90 miles across from the island of Tiree in the west to Helensburgh in the east. It has six main towns, 25 inhabited islands and over 3,000 kilometres of coastline – more than the entire coastline of France.

Physically, Argyll and Bute is stunning. The claim to have the 'best environment' is not exaggerated. With wild and rugged countryside, mountains and lochs, the area supports the most extensive range of flora and fauna in the UK. Access to this spectacular landscape is provided for through paths for a range of abilities, including those of limited mobility.

The paths in this book highlight some of the best scenery, wildlife and heritage that Argyll and Bute has to offer, from the historical interest and scenery of the Crinan Canal, to the unique flora and fauna of Loch Barnluasgan and Mòine Mhòr.

For general enquiries about outdoor access or for reporting of outdoor access issues in Argyll & Bute, please contact the Outdoor Access Officer on 01546 604301.

This section also covers Loch Lomond & The Trossachs National Park, where the magnificent landscape has fired the imagination of writers and artists for centuries. It embraces the deep waters of Loch Lomond, the wild glens of the Trossachs, Breadalbane's high mountains and the sheltered sea lochs of the Argyll Forest. The National Park feels worlds apart from the bustle of city life. Yet it is less than an hour from Glasgow and not much more from Edinburgh. There is something for everyone to enjoy in Scotland's first National Park. Whatever the weather, Loch Lomond and The Trossachs provide a stunning backdrop to your visit. The National Park provides a wide range of recreational opportunities from easy and safe off-road cycles along the network cycle paths and forest tracks. The riverside paths at Aberfoyle, Luss and Balloch are particularly good for wheelchair users looking for low gradients and smooth surfaces, and there are plenty of options in the surrounding areas for the more adventurous.

For general enquiries about access or for reporting access issues in the National Park, contact the Senior Access Officer on 01389 722600, or visit www.lochlomond-trossachs.org

Argyll, Loch Lomond and the Trossachs

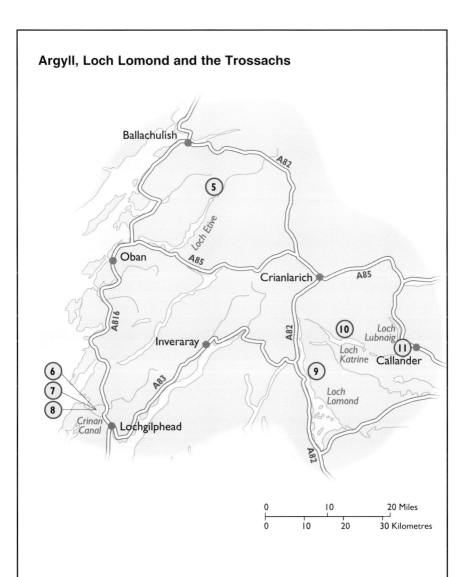

Trail Number	Name	Distance (Miles/KM)
5	Glen Etive	12/19
6	Mòine Mhòr	2/3
7	Crinan Canal	4/6
8	Loch Barnluasgan	2/3
9	Rowardennan	6/10
10	Loch Katrine	7/11
11	Callander to Strathyre	7/11

5 Glen Etive

Glen Etive, which is owned by the National Trust for Scotland, is very typical of the long, high-sided glens to be found on the West Coast of Scotland. If you're seeking that 'get-away-from-it-all' experience then you'll find it here. It has a tarmac, single track road that ends abruptly at Loch Etive. Consequently, traffic is minimal and you can park on the verge anywhere along its 12 miles (24 miles return). It follows the River Etive which is rarely out of earshot and if you reach the end you are rewarded with a beautiful view. But remember the 12-mile return journey, that is, unless you have someone who will come and pick you up.

My hillwalking friend who had suggested Loch Ordie, north of Dunkeld, also recommended Glen Etive. So imagine my delight when the Scottish Community Foundation ran their first Extra Challenge (for mobility-challenged people) in Glen Etive in 2004. Our Extra Challenge took place along the first 6 miles of Glen Etive. The weather was fairly bleak, but this did not stop us from having a marvellous experience of supported rambling which ended in a jamboree of medals, photos, massages, home baking, soup and burgers, all sponsored by IBM. Details of the event can be viewed on www.caledonianchallenge.com/extra/. The following year, 2005, the Extra Challenge was upgraded and took place not only on the day of the Caledonian Challenge but on a section of the West Highland Way itself, alongside the able-bodied competitors.

FURTHER INFORMATION

Scottish Natural Heritage Area Office, The Governor's House, The Parade, Fort William PH33 6BA: 01397 704716
Highland Access Officer: 01397 707050
NTS Visitor Centre, Glencoe: www.nts.org.uk or www.undiscoveredscotland.co.uk/glencoe/visitorcentre/

FACT FILE

Map	Ordnance Survey Landranger Sheets 41 & 50
Start	Glen Etive (NN 246548)
Finish	Loch Etive (NN 108450)
Parking	On verge of road anywhere
Toilets	Green Wellie Shop, Tyndrum W/C (R); NTS Visitor Centre, Glencoe W/C
Distance	12 miles / 19.5 km each way
Landscape	Hills / river / loch

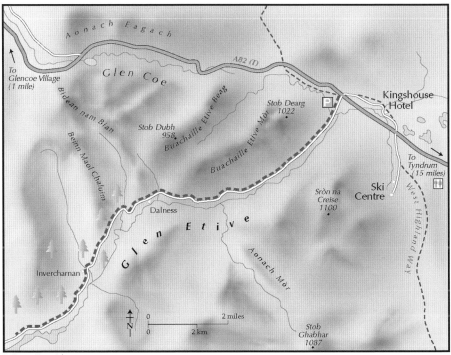

© Crown Copyright

View from the road, Glen Etive

6 Mòine Mhòr

Although it is five years since I first visited this area it seems like yesterday. A group of six disabled ramblers plus four volunteers met up with Hugh Fife, a great activist for disabled access working for Reforesting Scotland. We rambled from the car park and picnic site alongside the B8025, half-way between Kilmartin and Bellanoch. There is a useful information board at this point where copies of the leaflet 'Follow the Tileworks Trail' are usually available. The view from the duckboard spans an expanse of moss and draws the eye towards the isolated hill-fort of Dunadd, once the centre of the ancient kingdom of Dalriada. There is an interpretation point here. Down at bog level look out for hen harriers and curlews, as well as an impressive range of dragonflies in summer.

Walk towards Bellanoch on the quiet B8025. From up on the Crinan Canal towpath to Cairnbaan you can see the waterlogged system of pools and bogs alongside the gentle twists and turns of the River Add. Mòine Mhòr means 'the Great Moss' and you can see why.

Scottish Natural Heritage (SNH) manages this National Nature Reserve and many other extraordinary places, for the benefit of both wildlife and people. The remarkable landscapes, animals and plants which they protect can be enjoyed by everyone.

FURTHER INFORMATION

British Waterways Highland Canals' Customer Service Manager: 01463 725500
SNH, Kilmory Industrial Estate, Lochgilphead, Argyll PA31 8RR: 01546 604301
Access Officer: 01546 604228

FACT FILE

Map	Ordnance Survey Landranger Sheet 55
Start and Finish	Car Park on B8025 (NM 826959)
Parking	Small car park at picnic site B8025
	Bridge at Crinan Canal on B8025
Toilets	Lochgilphead shore front W/C; Crinan, walk in, one step; Bellanoch BW Toilet. Key-purchase through https://www.chandleryshop.com
Distance	4 miles / 6.5 km return
Landscape	National Nature Reserve forest / canal / wetland

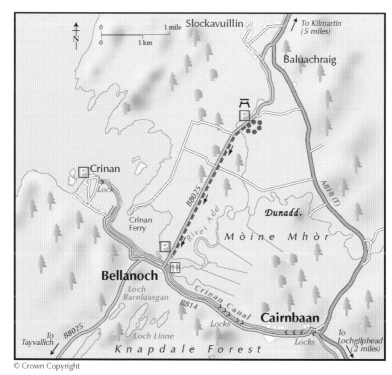

© Crown Copyright

Murky day over Mòine Mhòr

7 Crinan Canal

Another of the walks we did with Hugh Fife was beside the Crinan Canal. We rambled along its towpath from the bridge near Bellanoch to Crinan locks where we sat on the grass enjoying our lunch while watching the boats work through the locks. In 2005 I returned to Crinan for a meeting of the British Waterways Scotland Group on which I sat as a voice for towpath users. In the wettest of conditions I went in my electric wheelchair from Cairnbaan to Bellanoch.

I love towpath rambling, especially when there is water on both sides, and the Crinan Canal offers just this. The Crinan sea loch to the north was spectacular and out came our cameras to help us remember. There were many interesting boats moored along the way including *The Vital Spark,* which, on my more recent visit, I learnt has been bought by a conservation group in Ayrshire.

The Crinan Canal was constructed under the supervision of John Rennie between 1793 and 1801. The canal is only 9 miles long, from Crinan to Ardrishaig, but it saved boats having to make a journey of over 100 miles round the Mull of Kintyre and up the Firth of Clyde and Loch Fyne. The canal has 15 locks.

Unfortunately, the pedestrian bridges at canal locks are not accessible by wheelchair and so we had to return the 1.5 miles to Bellanoch.

FURTHER INFORMATION

British Waterways Highland Canals' Customer Service Manager: 01463 725500 enquiries.hq@britishwaterways.co.uk
Access Officer: 01546 604301

FACT FILE

Map	Ordnance Survey Landranger Sheet 55
Start	Bellanoch (NM 805925)
Parking	Bridge at Crinan Canal on B8025; Cairnbaan
Toilets	Lochgilphead shore front W/C; Crinan, walk in, one step; Bellanoch BW Toilets. Key-purchase through https://www.chandleryshop.com
Distance	3 miles / 5 km return (+ 4 miles / 6.5 km return to Cairnbaan)
Landscape	Waterscape / mountains / forest

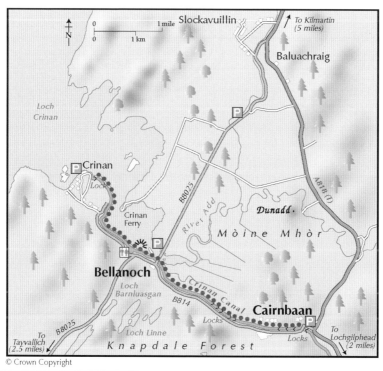

© Crown Copyright

Rambling along Crinan Canal

8 Loch Barnluasgan

The third ramble with Hugh Fife was at Loch Barnluasgan, and what a lovely surprise it was. Take the B8025 south from Bellanoch for a mile and park at the Forestry Commission's Forest Walks' car park. From here, take the path north along the left side of Loch Barnluasgan. All along the way there are attractive, waist-high interpretative points with easily accessible flaps and hands-on gadgetry (e.g. magnifier). Near the top end of the loch take the path veering left. This is slightly steeper and rougher terrain for which I recommend a scooter. It is well worth the effort because as you carry on up and round the corner you will be rewarded by a wonderful view towards the Crinan Canal and Mòine Mhòr (Trails 6 & 7).

On returning, there is another lovely view (front book cover). As you reach Loch Barnluasgan, turn left to the top end where there is a bird hide. During our visit Hugh went to the loch side and fished out a leech. Never having seen a leech before, I was impressed to find one in Scotland. Carry on round the far side of the loch and you will return to the car park. You may wish to extend your time in the area, in which case a further linear walk to Loch Coille-Bharr (2 miles return) is worthwhile if you have a scooter.

The Forestry Commission Information Board states that 'These woodlands will be protected under European law and Forest Enterprise manages and conserves its varied special habitats for the benefit of future generations.'

FURTHER INFORMATION

Forestry Commission Scotland (West Argyll): 01546 602518
west.argyll.fd@forestry.gsi.gov.uk
Access Officer: 01546 604301 or enquiries@argyll-bute.gov.uk

FACT FILE

Map	Ordnance Survey Landranger Sheet 55
Start and Finish	Loch Barnluasgan car park (NM 790910)
Parking	Forest Walk Centre
Toilets	Lochgilphead shore front W/C; Crinan, walk in, one step; Bellanoch BW Toilet Block. Key-purchase through https://www.chandleryshop.com
Distance	2 miles / 3 km return (+ 2 miles / 3 km return to Loch Barnluasgan
Landscape	Waterscape / hills / forest

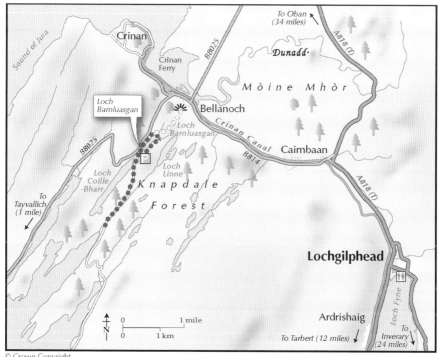

© Crown Copyright

Habitat for plant and insect life

9 Rowardennan

I have for many years been tantalised by the West Highland Way (WHW). In the late 1980s my husband and brother walked it together. In 2004 and 2005 my daughters ran it in the Caledonian Challenge. Oh how I wanted to do at least a part of it. At last my opportunity came. In August 2005 I was holidaying in Rowardennan Youth Hostel which is situated on the WHW and used by many walkers as an overnight stop. Needless to say, perched on my scooter, off I went exploring. Heading south, I took the unlisted road towards Balmaha. Half a mile later at the The Clansman pub, I followed the WHW up a narrow, steep hill. Unfortunately, this proved a little too challenging and I had to return to the safety of tarmac. I continued down the road and after a further ½ mile, I once again meandered off towards the loch side and found the other side of the hill and the WHW. These also were too steep.

And so I continued, for 5 miles down the unlisted road, taking occasional detours to explore more accessible paths on the WHW. However, I had the northern route of the WHW still to explore.

At last I found what I consider 'proper rambling' on the WHW. For a mile my wheels took me blissfully along a stable, flat trail running along the side of Loch Lomond. Unfortunately, at Ptarmigan Lodge, not only does the path become steep (1:7) but a Forest Enterprise gate, with a, sadly, too-small kissing gate, was a barrier. By this time I had met up with the National Trust for Scotland Ranger and he suggested that I could possibly continue for at least another mile of the WHW.

The Ranger advises that for car access through the gate it is best to phone a couple of days before a visit. With prior arrangement guides can accompany visitors for a time to help inform them about many aspects of the Rowardennan area. Donations accepted!

FURTHER INFORMATION

National Trust for Scotland: Ben Lomond Ranger 01360 870224
www.nts.org.uk

FACT FILE	
Map	Ordnance Survey Landranger Sheet 56
Start and Finish	Rowardennan Youth Hostel (NS 360989)
Parking	NTS Ranger Centre by arrangement
Toilets	NTS Ranger Centre W/C accessible
Distance	6 miles / 9.5 km (or more)
Landscape	Waterscape / Ben Lomond / forest

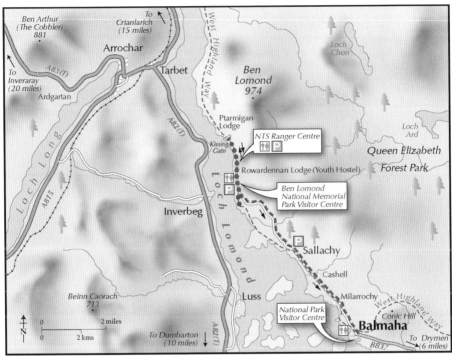

The following labels appear on the map:

Ben Arthur
(The Cobbler)
881

To
Crianlarich
(15 miles)

West Highland Way

Arrochar

Tarbet

To
Inveraray
(20 miles)

Ardgartan

A83(T)

A82(T)

Loch
Chon

Ben
Lomond
974

Loch
Ard

Ptarmigan
Lodge

NTS Ranger Centre

Queen Elizabeth
Forest Park

Kissing
Gate

Rowardennan Lodge (Youth Hostel)

Ben Lomond
National Memorial
Park Visitor Centre

Loch Long

A815

Inverbeg

Loch Lomond

Sallachy

Cashell

Beinn Caorach
713

Luss

Milarrochy

West Highland Way

National Park
Visitor Centre

Conic Hill

Balmaha

0   2 miles

N

0   2 kms

A82(T)

To Dumbarton
(10 miles)

B837

To Drymen
(6 miles)

West Highland Way at Rowardennan

10 Loch Katrine

Loch Katrine is part of Loch Lomond and The Trossachs National Park. The dramatic scenery around Loch Katrine inspired the setting of Sir Walter Scott's book, *The Lady of the Lake,* and it was his colourful description that first attracted tourists to Scotland. The name Loch Katrine is from the Gaelic *cateran*, meaning a Highland robber. The loch is just under 10 miles long, and 1 mile across at the widest part and supplies the City of Glasgow with approximately 85 million gallons of water per day.

For the rambler with wheels, whether a wheelchair, scooter or pram, the tarmac road along the north side is ideal. This is a service road for the water authority and access to a couple of houses. The only traffic of any significance is pedestrians and cyclists. The car park at Trossachs Pier is ample with several designated disabled bays and a toilet accessible by wheelchair but not scooter. A magnificent old Scottish building has been converted into the Captain's Rest Cafe and Gift Shop. An easy, short ramble with views of water, forest and mountains on a well-surfaced and reasonably flat road will take you to Brenachoille Point, a lovely picnic spot. A further 5 miles will reward you with a view back down the loch or over towards Ben Lomond. To carry on further entails gradients of more than 1:10. The three marked deer grids have accessible side gates which are difficult to manipulate from sitting position.

If you have enough energy/power this trail would provide a great day out. In theory, you could ramble the 10 miles to the North West point and 3 miles back along the south road to Stronachlachar Pier and take the afternoon boat back to Trossachs Pier. The steamship, *Sir Walter Scott,* has wheelchair access on to the top deck. There is no access to the cabins below deck where the toilet facilities and cafe/bar are. There was, however, a wheelchair lift to the Captain's Rest at Trossachs Pier which is accessed from outside.

FURTHER INFORMATION

www.lochlomond-trossachs.org

FACT FILE

Map	Ordnance Survey Landranger Sheets 56 and 57
Start and Finish	Trossachs Pier (NN 495072).
Parking	Trossachs Pier
Toilets	Trossachs Pier Radar W/C (L)
Distance	7 miles / 11 km (or more)
Landscape	Waterscape / mountains / forest

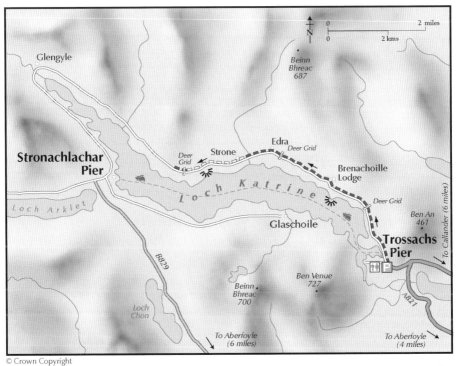

Loch Katrine and the hills of the Trossachs

11 Callander to Strathyre

Argyll, Loch Lomond & The Trossachs

In July 2005 we had friends visiting from London and together we decided to attempt Schiehallion, a Munro of 1,083 metres. After a great morning on this mountain we motored south to Strathyre to complete a further 6 miles of National Cycle Route 7, 'Callander to Strathyre', but in reverse, i.e. from Strathyre heading south. My husband dropped off my girlfriend and myself (with scooter) and off we set. After a mile of reasonable path we were delighted by a lovely view down Loch Lubnaig. Be warned: the path then became narrow and unstable and the descent to the loch side included a hairpin bend. Unfortunately, my scooter did not cope with a hidden boulder and threw me out on to the bracken! Five minutes of expert handling of both me and my scooter and my friend had us back on the path to Callander. After this section of narrow, challenging track, the remaining 4 miles along the edge of Loch Lubnaig were very pleasant and without incident.

As there are gates for stock control and some of the steps on to the sheep grids at the Strathyre end are inaccessible without a small ramp, I would recommend Cycle Route 7 from Callander north for anything up to 6 miles. Or perhaps you would prefer a short 1-mile ramble from Strathyre to the lovely viewpoint looking down Loch Lubnaig.

FURTHER INFORMATION

Sustrans: www.nationalcyclenetwork.org.uk

FACT FILE

Map	Ordnance Survey Landranger Sheet 57
Start	Strathyre (NN 623080)
Finish	Callander (NN 558171)
Parking	Callander Riverside car park; Strathyre, on road near school
Toilets	Callander main car park north of A84 radar W/C (L)
Distance	7 miles / 11 km one way
Landscape	River / loch / mountains / forest

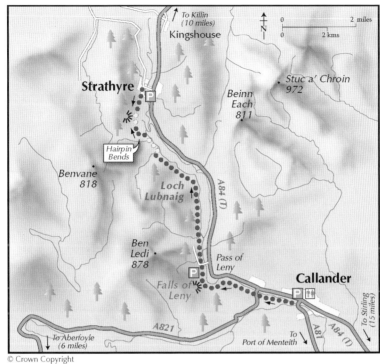

View of Loch Lubnaig

CAIRNGORMS NATIONAL PARK

The Cairngorms National Park is Britain's largest. At its heart is an area of wild, high land that is as much arctic as Scottish in nature. Heather moor, native pinewoods and traditionally managed farmland flank this mountain core. Lochs containing pure water are found throughout the Park and these feed three major rivers, the Dee, Don and Spey. This combination of special habitats in close proximity is unique in Britain and is part of the reason the Park contains a quarter of our endangered species. Scottish crossbill, golden eagle, osprey, dotterel, capercaillie and crested tit are just a few of the bird species found here.

The Cairngorms have long been known as an area that could offer challenges for mountaineers and climbers. However, it is perhaps less well known that the lower ground around the mountains contains a network of easily accessed paths. These routes offer stunning views of the mountains while bringing you close to the wildlife and geology of the area.

For the first time this publication brings together twelve walks from around the Park that give visitors with reduced mobility the chance to see the best that the Cairngorms National Park has to offer.

The Cairngorms National Park Authority was established in 2003 to ensure that partners throughout the area work collectively to achieve the aims of the national park. The Authority is the Local Outdoor Access Authority for the area.

For general enquiries about outdoor access or for reporting outdoor access issues in the Park, please contact the Outdoor Access Officer on 01479 873535 or visit www.cairngorms.co.uk.

Cairngorms National Park

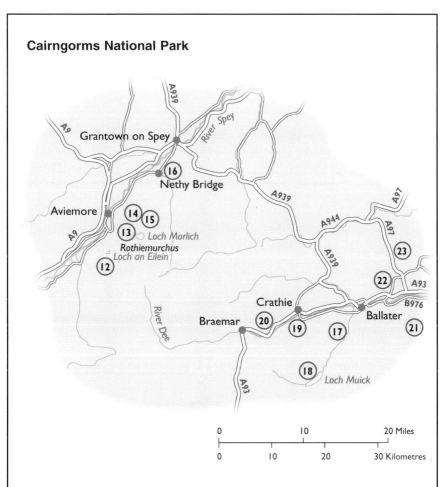

Trail Number	Name	Distance (Miles/Km)
12	Loch an Eilein	3/5
13	Loch Morlich	4 or 2.5 / 6 or 4
14	Badaguish	1.5 or 2 / 2 or 3
15	Glenmore Forest	4/6
16	Nethy Bridge	3 or 2.5 / 5 or 4
17	Balmoral Estate	7/11
18	Loch Muick	6/10
19	Crathie	2/3
20	Invercauld	3/5
21	Glen Tanar	Various 1-6 / 1.5-10
22	Cambus o' May	Various 1-6 / 1.5-10
23	Burn o' Vat	Various 1-6 / 1.5-10

12   Loch an Eilein

Rothiemurchus Estate offers a wide range of natural habitats. Woodlands of different kinds, wet and dry heaths, wetlands, grassland, river, stream and loch all provide a variety of locations where plants and animals can live.

James Page, a fellow disabled rambler, wrote of this walk: 'We set off down a minor road, then into the forest on a typical forest track. This was no rigidly structured symmetrical plantation of alien species; this was natural native woodland. Some of the younger trees on the outside leaned at an angle which showed the direction of the prevailing wind, but further in were some magnificent old pines, tall and straight, probably at least 250–300 years old. And there were cherry trees in bloom. Not the lollipop gene so beloved of suburbia, but real, gnarled and twisted old trees whose flowers add to their attraction but aren't worn like make-up. And then we came to the loch. You know the picture found on the lids of expensive boxes of chocolates, showing a background of mountains with some snow near the summit, perfectly reflected in the lake in the foreground, with beautiful trees at the edges and a brilliant blue sky above? Well, this must be where they took the photograph. It's not some expensive, idyllic resort, and it doesn't take a day and a half trekking to get there.'

If you still don't believe this place is magical, there's a part of the pathway where you're walking down to the loch and the burn is flowing towards you, uphill! And to cap it all, there's a ruined castle on an island. What more could you want?

FURTHER INFORMATION

The Badenoch & Strathspey Access Panel: 01479 811004
www.speyaccessguide.org
Rothiemurchus Estate: 01479 812345 www.rothiemurchus.net

FACT FILE

Map	Ordnance Survey Landranger Sheet 36
Start and Finish	Car park at NH 898084
Parking	Visitor Centre with Blue Badge
Toilets	Visitor Centre W/C (L); Rothiemurchus Visitor Centre W/C (L)
Distance	3 miles / 5 km circular
Landscape	Loch / woods / heath / castle

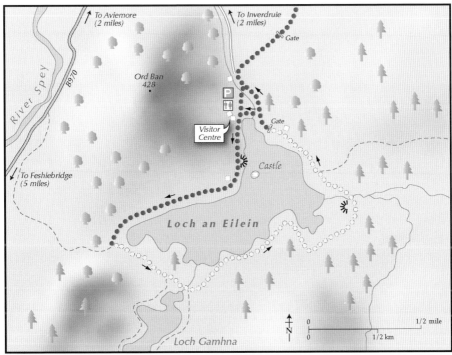

Ruined castle, Loch an Eilean

13 Loch Morlich

On our visit the ranger took us along the recently upgraded All Ability path to Loch Morlich and the surrounding area. We parked our cars in the Glenmore Forest Visitor Centre car park and carefully crossed the road towards the caravan park. The path meandered through the caravan park along tarmac roads until it met up with the waymarked All Ability path which officially starts at the car park 200 yards to the north of this point. The waymarked route continues on a stable, flat track to the loch side which in summer is a hive of water sports' activity. Nevertheless, if you continue quietly along the track many water birds may be spotted. This is a lovely path through the old Caledonian Forest with Scots pine towering above you.

The track ends at the road for Cairngorm skiing and the funicular railway, which means it can be busy. You now have a choice: to return by the same path (4 miles linear); to return by road (2½-mile circuit) or to cross the road, head south for less than ¼ mile and find the other track around the forest. For just over 400 yards it is known as Allt Mhòr Forest Trail. The trail then becomes steep and challenging and takes you on a round trip of a mile, approximately, before bringing you back to the road.

The Glenmore Forest Visitor Centre is well worth a visit and houses a good display area, shop, café and accessible toilet. It now has four scooters (4 wheel) for free loan from the Badenoch & Strathspey Community Transport Company which can be contacted on 01478 810004 from Monday to Friday during office hours. Please allow at least 24 hours notice.

FURTHER INFORMATION

Glenmore Forest Visitor Centre: Recreation Ranger 01479 861220
invernessfd@forestry.gsi.gov.uk
The Badenoch & Strathspey Access Panel 01479 811004
www.speyaccessguide.org
Rothiemurchus Estate: www.rothiemurchus.net

FACT FILE	
Map	Ordnance Survey Landranger Sheet 36
Start and Finish	Glenmore Forest Visitor Centre (NH 977099)
Parking	Visitor Centre
Toilets	Visitor Centre W/C (R)
Distance	Green: 4 miles / 6.5 km to road (including return)
	Green & Red: 2.5 miles / 4 km circular
Landscape	Loch side and old Caledonian Forest

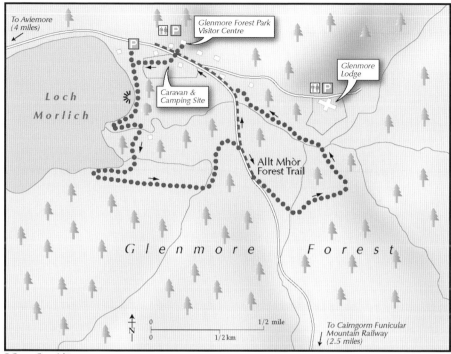

Within the map:

To Aviemore
(4 miles)

Glenmore Forest Park
Visitor Centre

Glenmore
Lodge

Caravan &
Camping Site

Loch
Morlich

Allt Mhòr
Forest Trail

G l e n m o r e   F o r e s t

0   1/2 mile
0   1/2 km
N

To Cairngorm Funicular
Mountain Railway
(2.5 miles)

Forest path near Loch Morlich

14 Badaguish

A group of us visited Badaguish Centre in summer 2003 and spent two nights in wonderful, newly built lodges. They were very spacious and housed eight persons. Two bedrooms were on the ground floor; one with ensuite had a roll-in, wet-floor shower and the other had a fully accessible toilet. The kitchen/dining area was large, accessible and very nicely furnished. For further information on the chalets see contact details below.

There are many moderate trails surrounding the Badaguish Centre. You can meander for miles along well-maintained Forestry Commission trails. Or why not take the high track to the Glenmore Forest Park Visitor Centre where you can enjoy excellent facilities including a shop, café and displays? You could then return by the lower green track which was reasonable in 2003 and had plans for further improvements. In 2005 I noticed these improvements had been completed but I did not test out this path.

In the summer months there is much water sport activity to observe on Loch Morlich. Car parking at the side of Loch Morlich is reasonable.

FURTHER INFORMATION

CNP Visitor Service: 01479 873535 www.cairngorms.co.uk
The Badenoch & Strathspey Access Panel 01479 811004
www.speyaccessguide.org
Badaguish Outdoor Centre: 01479 861285
Glenmore Forest Visitor Centre: Recreation Ranger 01479 861220 or
invernessfd@forestry.gsi.gov.uk

FACT FILE

Map	Ordnance Survey Landranger Sheet 36
Start and Finish	Badaguish (NH 956115)
	Visitor Centre (NH 977099) (off map)
Parking	Badaguish; Glenmore Forest Park Visitor Centre
Toilets	Badaguish – choice of accessibility; Visitor Centre W/C (R)
Distance	2 miles / 3 km circular, 1.5 miles to Visitor Centre
Landscape	Woodland

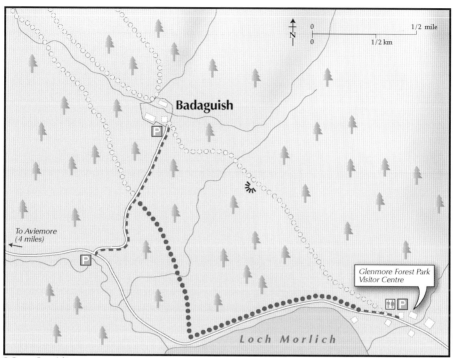

Water sports on Loch Morlich

15 Glenmore Forest

The route from Glenmore Forest Park Visitor Centre to An Lochan Uaine offers a good day out. The last ½ mile is quite challenging – and remember you have to come back the same way! The path continues over to Abernethy Forest (see Nethy Bridge map) but we were not equipped to test it.

When you leave the Visitor Centre you pass the Cairngorm Reindeer Centre, so look left and you might catch a glimpse of these majestic creatures. The first mile is a long, gentle climb on a quiet road after which the trail is moderately steep with a good surface which deteriorates gradually. Roots, stumps and ditches require more robust wheels.

All along the trail you are surrounded by trees whispering as you pass, but once at An Lochan Uaine a tranquil peace surrounds you. For me, water surrounded by mountains always seems to invoke a feeling of stillness and quiet beauty. Luckily, there was a good resting and turning place with views over the lochan. The water is a wonderful shade of green and the lochan is said to be the abode of fairies.

On the return journey we stopped at Glenmore Lodge which is run by Sport Scotland as a National Outdoor Training Centre for All Abilities. It is open all year. The lounge is upstairs but is accessible by lift and serves bar meals. It now has four scooters (4 wheel) for free loan from the Badenoch & Strathspey Community Transport Company which can be contacted on 01478 810004 from Monday to Friday during office hours. Please allow at least 24 hours notice.

FURTHER INFORMATION

The Badenoch & Strathspey Access Panel: 01479 811004
www.speyaccessguide.org
Glenmore Forest Visitor Centre: Recreation Ranger: 01479 861220
Glenmore Lodge 01479 861256 www.glenmorelodge.org.uk

FACT FILE

Map	Ordnance Survey Landranger Sheet 36
Start and Finish	Glenmore Forest Park Visitor Centre (NH 977099)
Parking	Glenmore Forest Visitor Centre & Glenmore Lodge
Toilets	Visitor Centre W/C (R); Glenmore Lodge – choice of accessibility
Distance	4 miles / 6.5 km circular
Landscape	Forest with views of mountains to north

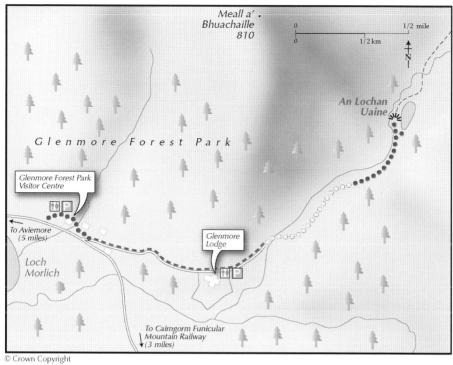

Within the map:

Meall a' Bhuachaille 810

0 ____ 1/2 mile
0 ____ 1/2 km

N

An Lochan Uaine

Glenmore Forest Park

Glenmore Forest Park Visitor Centre

To Aviemore (5 miles)

Loch Morlich

Glenmore Lodge

To Cairngorm Funicular Mountain Railway (3 miles)

Glenmore Forest

16 Nethy Bridge

The Scottish Disabled Ramblers was set up in the year 2000. By May 2001 we were so smitten with the idea of rambling in the Great Outdoors we decided to visit the Cairngorms National Park. This would necessitate staying overnight. Finding suitable accessible accommodation at reasonable cost was our first challenge. Fortunately, through previous contacts, I was able to source cottages and bed spaces at Nethy Bridge (see website below).

Nethy Bridge lies on the banks of the River Nethy and is within the CNP. There is an excellent network of waymarked trails and, as you can see from the map, most of the trails I followed were very accessible.

In Abernethy Forest, look around for examples of the Abernethy pine which were of exceptional quality and good for ships' masts, joinery, construction and railway sleepers.

Nethy Bridge is on the route of the Speyside Way path, which runs from Spey Bay to Aviemore. Not far away is Loch Garten (signposted from Boat of Garten), where the RSPB has a visitor centre. The loch is famous for its ospreys, which nest here each spring.

When we stayed in Nethy Bridge, at Forest Cottages, we discovered the forests to the north of the village and were tempted by the gate at the back garden. We found a pattern of paths, obviously used as shortcuts and by local people, but the majority were not wheel friendly. You might wish to explore these if you have a scooter but stay clear if you have small wheels.

FURTHER INFORMATION

The Badenoch & Strathspey Access Panel: 01479 811004
www.speyaccessguide.org
Explore Abernethy 01479 821565 www.exploreabernethy.com
Hostel / cottages: 01479821642 www.forestcottages.com

FACT FILE	
Map	Ordnance Survey Landranger Sheet 36
Start and Finish	Nethy Bridge Community Centre (NH 102206)
Parking	Community Centre
Toilets	Adjacent to Community Centre W/C (L) radar
Distance	Abernethy Forest: 3 miles / 5 km circular
	Riverside: 2.5 miles / 4 km circular
Landscape	River / woodland

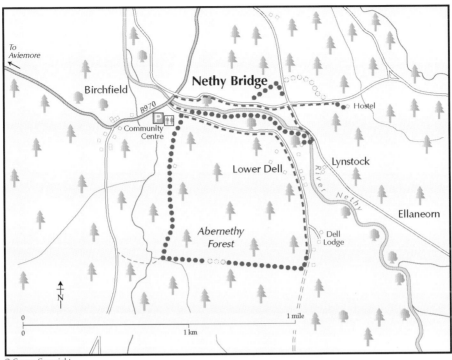

Swimming pool

17 Balmoral Estate

Ballater Royal Deeside Ltd is a charitable organisation which, amongst other things, organises a walking week towards the end of May every year. Since 2002 it has also included three All Ability walks during each walking festival. I have been very fortunate in being asked to liaise with the organisers, during the winter months prior to the walking week, in order to assess the suitability of the chosen walks. In 2005 the Resident Factor of Balmoral Estate advised on a trail from Spittal of Glenmuick to Mill of Sterin.

Park at Spittal car park and, before you set off, take the opportunity to visit the small but fascinating Visitor Centre. From there, take the estate track towards Lochnagar, which you will see in front of you and on your left. The land here is just above the tree line on fairly flat, open moorland which can attract blustery weather so make sure you have appropriate outdoor clothing. Wildlife, from raptors to tiny wildflowers, is here in abundance

Once across the moorland, take the path right and continue until you come to a gate with pedestrian/wheelchair access on its left. Follow the River Muick, stopping at Linn of Muick waterfall and ask your more able companion to take a photo as this is the only way you'll see it! However, you will hear it. The surrounding wooded area is a very pleasant spot for a short break before continuing down to the Cock's Neck at Mill of Sterin where the tarmac road allows for easy pick-up by car.

FURTHER INFORMATION

Balmoral Estate: Ranger 01339 742534 www.balmoralcastle.com
Ballater Royal Deeside Ltd: 01339 755467

FACT FILE

Map	Ordnance Survey Landranger Sheet 44
Start	Spittal of Glenmuick (NO 309849)
Finish	Mill of Sterin (NO 349928)
Parking	Spittal of Glenmuick
Toilets	Spittal of Glenmuick, walk in only
	Ballater car park W/C (L) Radar
Distance	7 miles / 11 km one way
Landscape	Moorland / woodland / river

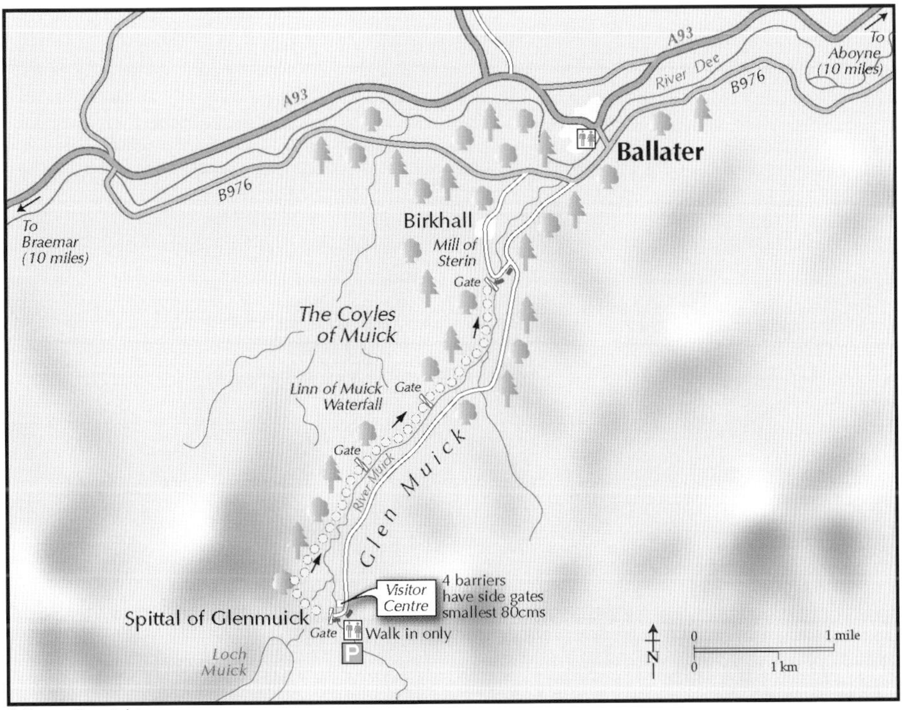
A93
River Dee
B976
To Aboyne (10 miles)
Ballater
A93
B976
To Braemar (10 miles)
Birkhall
Mill of Sterin
Gate
The Coyles of Muick
Linn of Muick Waterfall
Gate
Gate
River Muick
Glen Muick
Visitor Centre
4 barriers have side gates smallest 80cms
Spittal of Glenmuick
Gate
Walk in only
P
Loch Muick
N
0
1 mile
0
1 km

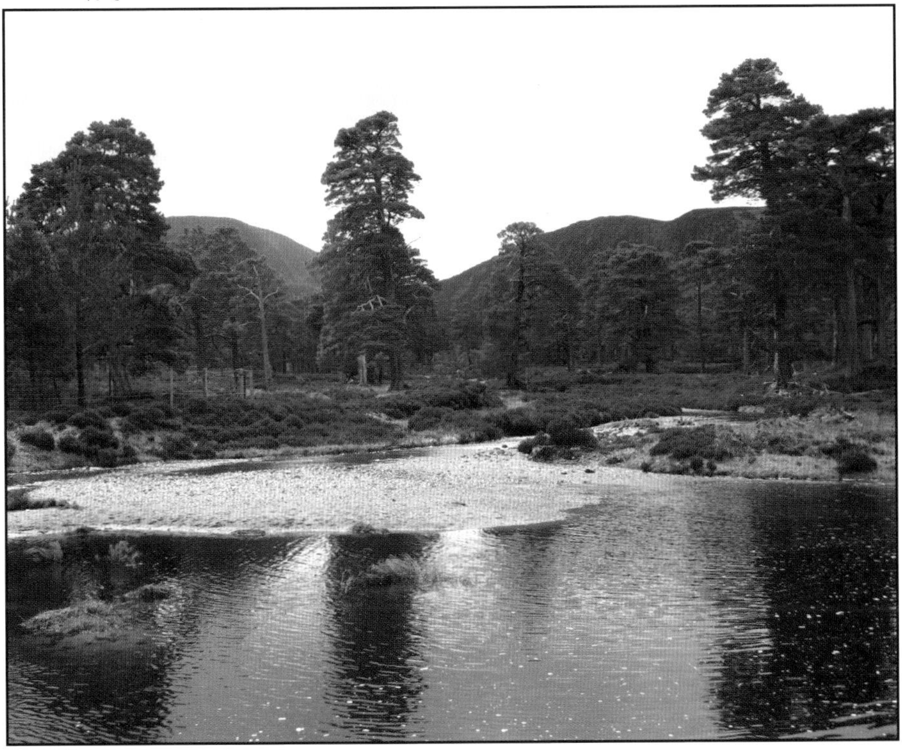

Pool on Balmoral Estate

18 Loch Muick

I have visited Loch Muick on three occasions and always find it awesome. I think this is because the lack of trees makes it feel remote and vast. The mountains on either side and in front of you on the way out are not Munros but they are well above the tree line and quite spectacular.

The weather in such places is always unpredictable and you can start out in sunshine only to be caught ten minutes later in a sudden drop in temperature or even stormy weather. So be prepared with warm and waterproof clothing.

The track is wide but rutted in places. If you get as far as Glas-allt-Sheil you will be rewarded as here you find the picnic house of Queen Victoria. It is not open for viewing and on my last visit it was boarded up. Surrounded by a beautiful little copse on the south-west end of Loch Muick, it is sheltered from the prevailing winds. Queen Victoria and Prince Albert often picnicked here, and after the Prince died, the Queen had the house built so that she could continue visiting the spot. She called it her 'Widow's House'. It is easy to see why it meant so much to her, for it really is a lovely place.

On your return, which will probably be late afternoon, keep your eyes open as deer often come down at this time of day to graze on the more lush grasses at the north-east end of the loch. The Estate has been planting small areas with trees along the path here.

The name 'Muick' derives from a Gaelic word meaning 'pigs' so there might have been wild boar in the area at one time. You will not of course see any today but you may well see the deer. 'Spittal' comes from a word for a hospice or shelter, and there was such a place here as this point was on a route used by drovers.

FURTHER INFORMATION

Ballater Royal Deeside Ltd: 01339 755467
Balmoral Estate Ranger: 01339 745234 www.balmoralcastle.com

FACT FILE

Map	Ordnance Survey Landranger Sheet 44
Start and Finish	Spittal of Glen Muick (NO 308850)
Parking	Spittal of Glen Muick
Toilets	Spittal of Glen Muick, walk in; Ballater car park W/C (L) radar
Distance	6 miles / 9.5 km return
Landscape	Open heath / loch side / high mountains

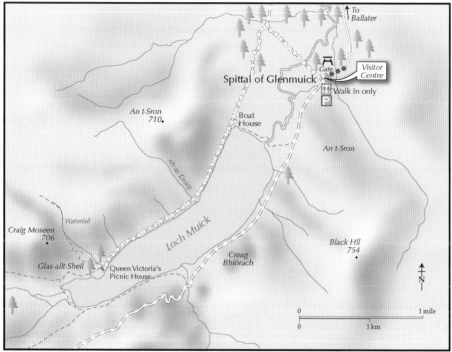

Within the map:

To
Ballater

Spittal of Glenmuick

Gate

Visitor
Centre

Walk in only

An t-Sron
710

Boat
House

An t-Sron

Alt na Deasg

Craig Moseen
706

Waterfall

Loch Muick

Black Hll
754

Glas-allt-Sheil

Queen Victoria's
Picnic House

Creag
Bhiòrach

N

0   1 mile
0   1 km

Silver birch in Glen Muick

19 Crathie

When rambling around Crathie, a visit to Crathie Church, famous for its royal visitors, is well worth taking.

As parking at the church car park involves crossing the busy A93, I would advise using the ample parking spaces on the south side of the A93. Head towards Balmoral Castle, but instead of turning in at the splendid gates, turn left and take the quiet road which follows the golf course on the banks of the River Dee. Less than a mile further on you will spot a white pedestrian bridge which takes you back over the river. To quote James Page: 'Giant flies were rising from the river and doing a drunken swirl all over the place. Stones in the river which had been underwater the day before were now basking in June sunshine. The young river was doing its urgent, there's-no-time-to-hang-about stuff.' Follow the path around and back towards your car. On your left there is the manse, then Crathie Opportunity Holidays and then a graveyard.

Having stayed at Crathie Opportunity Holidays on several occasions, I have come to love this route. I always find water very peaceful and tranquil, even when fast flowing, but here it moves slowly along, attracting birds and wildlife along its way. Over the years I have seen many frequent wildlife visitors here including a heron and a red squirrel. For a very good self-service meal the restaurant at Balmoral Castle is hard to beat. There are two accessible toilets and a busy shop.

FURTHER INFORMATION

Balmoral Estate Ranger: 01339 742534 www.balmoralcastle.com
Ballater Royal Deeside Ltd: 01339 755467
Crathie Opportunity Centre: 01339 742100 www.crathieholidays.org.uk

---

FACT FILE	
Map	Ordnance Survey Landranger Sheet 44
Start and Finish	Information & Car Park (NO 265949)
	Balmoral Castle car park (NO 255951)
Parking	Information car park; Balmoral Castle car park
Toilets	Information kiosk (at Crathie car park) W/C (L) 9.30-5.00 summer season only; Balmoral Castle café (R&L); Ballater car park W/C (L) radar
Distance	2 miles / 3 km circular
Landscape	Riverside, crossing on 2 bridges.

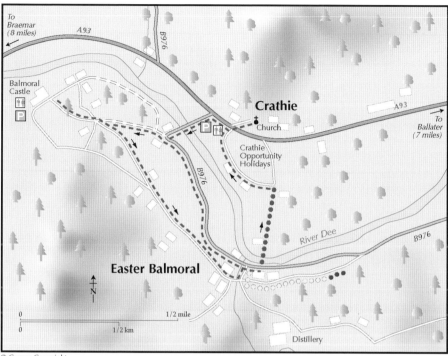

To
Braemar
(8 miles)

A93

B976

Balmoral
Castle

P

Crathie

Church

Crathie
Opportunity
Holidays

A93

To
Ballater
(7 miles)

P

B976

River Dee

B976

Easter Balmoral

N

0   1/2 mile

0
1/2 km

Distillery

Balmoral Castle

Invercauld Estate has many paths and the one suggested by the Estate Manager for wheelchair rambling runs parallel to the A93. Nevertheless, as it is hidden behind a low ridge, you can enjoy the fresh air, the rural atmosphere and listen to the birds without being aware of it. A scooter gives a more comfortable ramble because although the path is flat, the surface is variable.

This is a good linear walk. There is an opportunity to park at either end where there are toilets within sight of your car. However, the short distance of A93 to Inver Hotel requires a walking escort. Many people object to returning along the same path but I always find different things to see on the way back. By parking at Keiloch and returning there you can enjoy a 6-mile ramble. Most of the route is forested but with good views of grazing fields to the north. The countryside changes as you reach the Inver end. The small burn offers a more gentle and verdant feel and the tarmac road is a relief for those who have ventured this far without a comfortable scooter!

The Invercauld Estate is very extensive and stretches a long way back into the mountains, reaching to the summits of Beinn a' Bhùird and Ben Avon. The estate has been owned by the Farquharson family for centuries and they still live at Invercauld House.

FURTHER INFORMATION

Ballater Royal Deeside Ltd: 01339 755467

FACT FILE	
Map	Ordnance Survey Landranger Sheets 43 & 44
Start and Finish	Invercauld Estate car park (NO 188911)
Pick-up Point	Inver (NO 234938)
Parking	Invercauld Estate (£2); Inver Hotel (customers only); Inver (on road, 1 or 2 spaces)
Toilets	Invercauld Estate car park, walk in; Information kiosk (at Crathie car park) W/C (L) 9.30–5.00 p.m. summer season only; Balmoral Castle café W/C (R&L); Ballater car park W/C (L) radar
Distance	3 miles / 5 km one way
Landscape	Forest / rough grazing

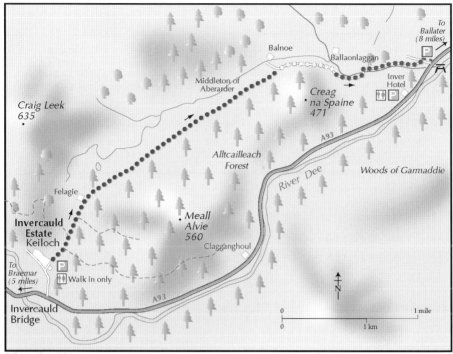

© Crown Copyright

Scots Pine on the Invercauld Estate

21 Glen Tanar

At the Glen Tanar Estate, the River Tanar, the Forest of Glen Tanar, Glen Tanar House and Home Farm, St Lesmo Church and a Visitor Centre are within rambling distance of each other. All will add interest to your visit. If you are lucky enough to secure a guided walk then the history of the area will raise your eyebrows. One of the Lairds, a man called William Cunliffe Brooks, was a great inventor, discovering ways of tapping into naturally occurring sources of water power. St Lesmo Church is an Episcopalian church which is shared by other denominations for weddings.

There are trails on either side of the River Tanar offering good rambles which can be accessed from Brig of Ess, the car park at the Visitor Centre, or the parking area near Glen Tanar House. If rambling from the latter, you go through a well-managed mixed forest where you can stop at bridges to listen to the rushing water. The path past St Lesmo Church to the visitor centre is shared with our friends, the sheep. I was very lucky to be helped to hose down my dung-covered wheels at Braeloine Visitor Centre. It is a small but friendly visitor centre full of interpretation boards. Outside there is a living maze. The bridge back to the car park is hump-backed and very challenging!

A blue road route can be followed from Brig of Ess to Braeloine Visitor Centre car park. If you want to return to Brig of Ess by estate tracks, past the Fairy Loch, a telephone call for the combination number for the padlock at the gate at Brig o' Ess can be obtained from the ranger.

FURTHER INFORMATION

Glen Tanar Ranger Service: Braeloine Visitor Centre Tel: 01339 886072

FACT FILE

Map	Ordnance Survey Landranger Sheet 44
Start and Finish	Braeloine Visitor Centre (NO 480965)
Parking	Braeloine Visitor Centre (£2 – free Tuesday when closed)
Toilets	Visitor Centre small W/C (L); Ballater Car Park W/C (L) radar
Distance	Various
Landscape	Old, well-managed forest / riverside path and high viewpoint / possible sightings of deer

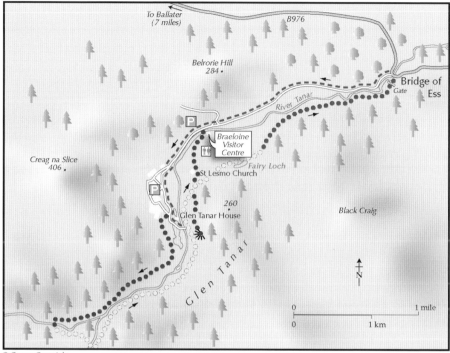

Fairy Loch, Glen Tanar Estate

22   Cambus o' May

Cambus o' May has many paths of mixed levels of difficulty and provides a good day's rambling. One of these could be combined with a visit to Burn o' Vat, Trail 23, in one day but there would not be much time for contemplation.

Cambus o' May comes from from Camas a' Mhàigh – bend of the plain. It is an area with several houses and a former railway station beside a big bend in the Dee valley east of Ballater. It is a beautiful pinewood and offers a variety of tracks from Blue to Red. All paths are waymarked using Forestry Commission codes (NB: not the same colour coding as used by the author). There is an accessible board-walk stretching across the western loch where a quiet stillness evokes tranquillity and peace. Wildlife includes red squirrel, roe deer, crossbills and anthills. For most of the year the lochan offers habitat suitable for ampihibians.

Interpretive panels are sited at key points. It is well worth visiting the viewing area south of the official parking area as it offers very fine interpretation.

NB: The red, yellow and green symbols on the posts are signposts for walking routes, not indications of trail difficulty. Forestry Commission Scotland has to close parts of Cambus o' May from time to time, for timber harvesting work. Details of these closures and diversions are published on their website.

FURTHER INFORMATION

www.forestry.gov.uk

FACT FILE

Map	Ordnance Survey Landranger Sheet 44
Start and Finish	Cambus o' May (NO 405980)
Parking	P on map – at least 10 cars
Toilets	Ballater car park W/C (L)
	6 miles / 9.5 km rambling around
Distance	Forest: managed & ancient
Landscape	Water: river, loch & stagnant.

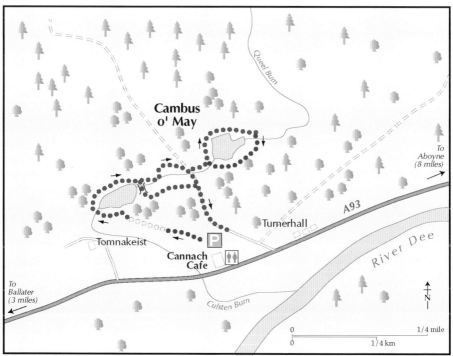

Cambus
o' May

Qureel Burn

To
Aboyne
(8 miles)

A93

Turnerhall

River Dee

Tomnakeist

P

Cannach
Cafe

To
Ballater
(3 miles)

Culsten Burn

N

| 0 | 1/4 mile |
| 0 | 1/4 km |

© Crown Copyright

Board-walk over western loch

23 Burn o' Vat

Cairngorms National Park (CNP)

Following a visit to Cambus o' May you might feel like exploring the area a little more. A mile and a half further along the A93 towards Aboyne turn left on to the B9119 and after a few bends you come upon a car park for the Burn o' Vat Visitor Centre. This includes a fully accessible toilet.

The path to the Vat is flat and of stable surface. It is beautiful and half way towards the Vat there is the most lovely riverside picnic area. The Vat (see photo) is itself, unfortunately, not accessible so ask your companion to take a photo for you.

On returning to the car park you might choose to climb to the high view point. This path is accessible but I would not attempt it in anything but a four-wheeled scooter as the path up is steep and winding. It is worth the climb, however, and ospreys can be seen in the spring and summer.

A circular track on the north side of Loch Kinord offers a good 3-mile ramble. You can start from Burn o' Vat car park but be careful crossing the road. There are several parking spots on the east approach to this walk where you could be collected or they could be used as the beginning of the circular green route. The most challenging bit of path is marked in red at the entry point P at the east of the loch for the circular route. This park is due to be upgraded.

FURTHER INFORMATION

SNH 01224 642863 www.nnr-scotland.org.uk

FACT FILE

Map	Ordnance Survey Landranger Sheet 44
Start and Finish	Burn o' Vat (NO 428997) or
	Loch Kinord (NO 449999)
Parking	Burn o' Vat Visitor Centre and east end of loch – at least 10 cars at both sites
Toilets	Burn o' Vat W/C (L); Ballater car park W/C (L)
Distance	6 miles / 9.5 km rambling around
Landscape	Forest: managed & ancient / Water: river & loch.

70   WALKING ON WHEELS

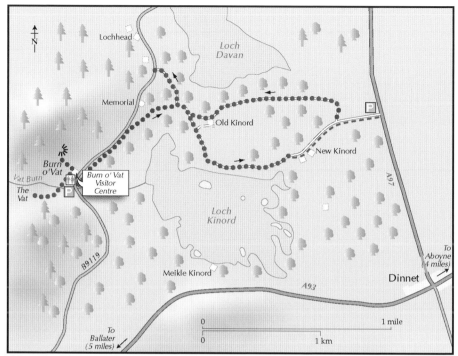

© Crown Copyright

The Vat

PERTH & KINROSS

Perth and Kinross is a County of spectacular differences; from Estuary to Munros and the botanical treasures of Ben Lawers and from the wooded height of Kinnoull Hill to the Black Wood of Rannoch. Numerous straths or valleys cross the County; the most notable being Strathtay, home of course to the magnificent River Tay. Widely accepted as Big Tree Country, Perth and Kinross has a long history of famous trees and people. Here you will find the oldest living tree in Europe – the Fortingal Yew; some of the tallest trees in Britain – the Dunkeld Douglas Firs and the parent (first planted) larches. Dunkeld is also the mainstay of Britain's commercial forestry industry. Notable plant collectors came from the area; David Douglas (who introduced the Douglas Fir) and Archibald Menzies, to name but two.

This collection of 'accessible for all walks', allows an insight to some of this landscape, history and wildlife without barriers to access. From exploration of riversides and woodlands, to 'hikes' up hills with stunning views, a taste of the real Perth and Kinross – the Big Tree Country – can be sampled.

The Council owns and manages sites across the County; the Den of Alyth, Kinnoull Hill Woodland Park and Lady Mary's Walk, to name but a few. For more information on access opportunities in Perth and Kinross, please contact Perth & Kinross Council Countryside Ranger Service on 01738 475393.

For general enquiries about outdoor access or for reporting outdoor access issues in Perth & Kinross, please contact the Outdoor Access Officer on 01738 475332.

Perth & Kinross

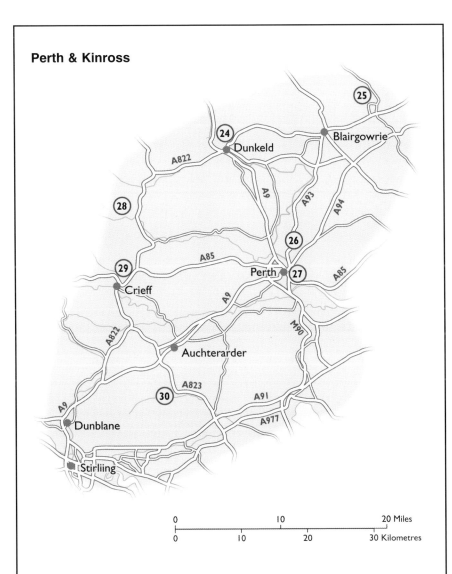

Trail Number	Name	Distance (Miles/Km)
24	Dunkeld (Hermitage & Loch Ordie)	1, 3 & 5 / 1.5, 5 & 8
25	Den of Alyth	1/1.5
26	Quarrymill	1/1.5
27	Kinnoull Hill & Deuchny Wood	2 & 3 / 3 & 5 circular
28	Glen Almond	5/8
29	Lady Mary's Walk, Crieff	4 & 6 / 6 & 10 circular
30	Glen Devon	3/5

24 Dunkeld, The Hermitage & Loch Ordie

Dunkeld is an old Cathedral town lying on the banks of the mighty River Tay. Across the water the larger buildings of Birnam reflect its rapid growth as a Victorian holiday resort with the coming of the railway. Although the main shopping street is full of specialist shops and restaurants, not many are accessible by wheels. But there are three very good routes out of Dunkeld, each offering a very different type of ramble.

The Hermitage (National Trust for Scotland): Head south over the bridge then turn right on to a path, following signs which take you under the A9 and then back alongside it before bringing you to the Hermitage trail. A fellow rambler friend, James Page, once wrote: 'The Hermitage was one place I really wanted to go to on a scooter. I'd been there often when both my legs were working and wanted to share the experience with others. When you pass under the road you've left all the world and its problems behind and when you arrive at the Hermitage you are witnessing the awesome power of the primeval element – water. Cleanse your mind of trivia like money and politics; be grateful you are not a fish trying to get to the spawning grounds.'

Loch Ordie: For a longer ramble, climbing higher into the hills, take the A923 north out of Dunkeld. After a sharp right turn, a quick left will take you to a Forestry Commission car park. Or you can, as I've done, go on the pavements in your wheels from the main Dunkeld car park. It is then a long, slow climb up through the forest to Loch Ordie, passing two other little lochs on the way. I believe it is possible to walk round the loch but I haven't done so: my scooter had had enough and we had to return.

FURTHER INFORMATION

Perth & Kinross Ranger Service: 01738 475393
Forestry Commission, Tay Forest District: 01350 727284
National Trust for Scotland Ranger Service: 01350 728641
Access Officer: 01738 475332

FACT FILE

Map	Ordnance Survey Landranger Sheet 53
Start and Finish	Car Park (NO 026427)
Parking	North Dunkeld (4 designated places)
Toilets	Car Park W/C (L) radar
Distance	2 miles / 3 km, 6 miles / 9.5 km & 10 miles / 16 km return
Landscape	Ancient wood / waterfall / moorland

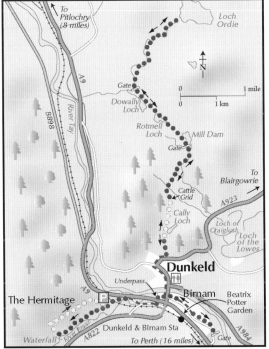

The Hermitage

25   Den of Alyth

In 2004 I was asked by Andrew Barrie, Perth & Kinross Countryside Ranger and Charles Dobb of the Alyth Environment Group to visit their newly upgraded path. A fellow wheelchair user from Blairgowrie joined us.

From the car park in Alyth you can head east or west for a round trip of less than a mile. The path going east is quite steep and a strong pair of arms would be needed in a manual wheelchair. However, once down at river level (marked A on the map) the path is reasonably flat with a good and stable surface. This trail offers a very picturesque trip amongst very tall trees with a view of the river. At the time of our visit the hairpin corner to take you back was very cambered and steep and in my opinion required a scooter. There was, however, talk of improving this corner for All Ability access. From here the short track back to the car park was uneven with occasional ruts and roots.

From river level (A) there is an alternative track leading east towards the village of Alyth which also runs parallel to the river and takes you through a large picnic and play area offering lots of fun for the family. Carrying on east to the gate you then have three choices: you can return by the same route; you can return by the B road or you can go into Alyth. The latter would extend your ramble by a further ½ mile towards Alyth.

FURTHER INFORMATION

Perth & Kinross Ranger Service: 01738 475393
Alyth Environment Group: 01828 633653

FACT FILE

Map	Ordnance Survey Landranger Sheet 53
Start and Finish	Car Park (NO 235488)
Parking	Alyth Car Park
Toilets	Blairgowrie W/C (R) radar; Alyth toilets not always open
Distance	1 mile / 1.5 km (2 miles / 3 km return)
Landscape	Woodland / river

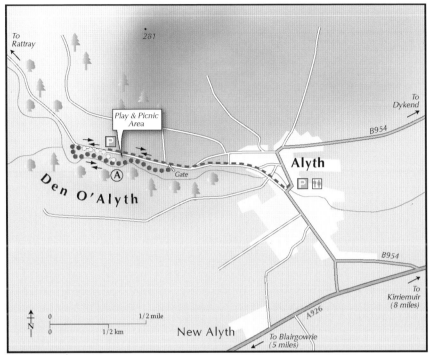

River-level path

26 Quarrymill

This is one of three short walks (only 2 miles return) in the book. I have included it because of its beauty and its history, both natural and built. I would advise a little research before you visit. Here is a taster: as its name suggests, Quarrymill was not always laid out with quiet woodland walks. The quarries were for stones for houses and the mills were built to grind bone meal, spin cotton and to extract starch from potatoes. Today's path leads to New Scone and Scone Old Parish Church, where stands a monument to the pioneering botanist David Douglas (1799–1834) who gave his name to the Douglas fir.

Quarrymill belongs to The Gannochy Trust, founded by A. K. Bell of Bell's Whisky in 1937. The Trust still manages the park and the coffee shop is operated by Macmillan Cancer Trust. The Scots pines found in the park were planted in the 1930s. The cones of these trees are essential to the survival of our native red squirrels and you may be lucky to catch sight of these beautiful animals. If you're visiting in the spring you will be rewarded with a carpet of bluebells underneath the beech trees. The Mill Pond has an ample supply of Canadian pondweed all year round, thus attracting mallards, moorhens and tufted ducks.

A good leaflet, *The Quarrymill Walk*: *Around Perth for Wheelchair Users* by Bob Bennett is available through the Fieldfare Trust.

FURTHER INFORMATION

Perth & Kinross Ranger Service: 01738 475393
The Fieldfare Trust: 01334 657708 www.fieldfare.org.uk

FACT FILE

Map	Ordnance Survey Landranger Sheet 53
Start and Finish	Car Park on A93 just north of Perth (NO 120252)
Parking	Quarrymill & Scone
Toilets	Coffee Shop W/C (L)
Distance	1 mile / 1.5 (2 miles / 3 km return)
Landscape	Ancient wood with river and pond

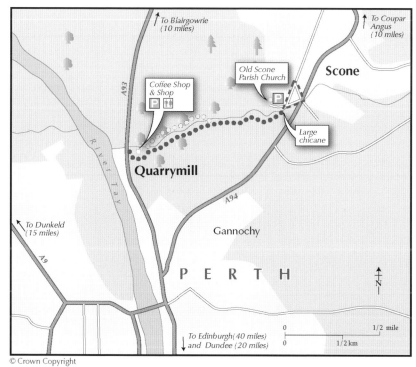

The map shows:

To Blairgowrie (10 miles)

To Coupar Angus (10 miles)

Scone

A93

Coffee Shop & Shop

Old Scone Parish Church

Quarrymill

Large chicane

River Tay

A94

To Dunkeld (15 miles)

A9

Gannochy

P E R T H

N

To Edinburgh (40 miles) and Dundee (20 miles)

0 .... 1/2 mile

0 .... 1/2 km

Viewpoint for water life

27 Kinnoull Hill & Deuchny Wood

I was thrilled to be asked by a Perth and Kinross Ranger in 2004 to accompany him on an access audit. We met in Jubilee Car Park and unloaded my scooter. We then had to cross a minor road but with someone to check for traffic this was not a problem. Once in the forest the paths were very good. Kinnoull Hill has a beautiful forest of birch and oak. The small stands of larch and Scots pine house red squirrels and roe deer. There is a short ½-mile circuit which is of blue standard. However, with strong muscles or a scooter a circuit of more than 2 miles is worth the effort. Near the summit is the 18th century Kinnoull Tower (see photo) built by the 9th Earl of Kinnoull as a landmark in imitation of the castles in the Rhine. From the seat at the Tower the view (marked on map) of the Ochil and Lomond Hills is spectacular. The cliffs here were formed by volcanic lava and provide favourable conditions for unusual plants but the area is designated as a Site of Special Scientific Interest. From here it is possible to return by exploring the different paths and we covered 3 miles easily.

Deuchny Hill has very good tracks, one built originally for the ancient kings and queens of Scotland for their journey between the Falkland and Scone Palaces. The tracks are well used by horses and cyclists so beware of traffic!

FURTHER INFORMATION

Perth & Kinross Ranger Service: 01738 475393
Forestry Commission Forester: 07712 750717

FACT FILE

Map	Ordnance Survey Landranger Sheet 53
Start and Finish	Jubilee Car Park, Kinnoull Hill (NO 145236)
Parking	Jubilee Car Park
Toilets	None at walk area; nearest at Rodney Fitness Centre, Dundee Rd., Perth (01738 630901) W/C (R)
Distance	2 miles / 3 km circular each walk
Landscape	Woodland / unusual plants / ancient route of kings / 18th century towers

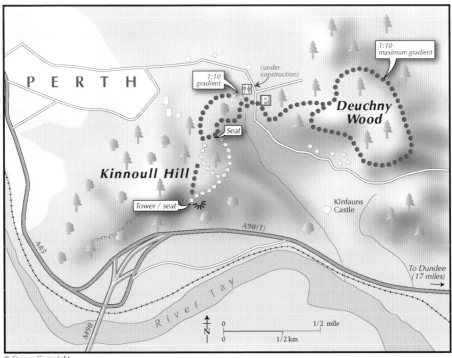

The following labels appear on the map:

P E R T H

Kinnoull Hill

Deuchny Wood

1:10 maximum gradient

(under construction)

1:10 gradient

Seat

Tower / seat

Kinfauns Castle

A90(T)

A85

M90

River Tay

To Dundee (17 miles)

0   1/2 mile
N
0   1/2 km

View of Kinnoull Hill and tower

28 Glen Almond

As can be seen by the lack of roads this 5-mile ramble (10 miles return) is away from civilisation. Well nearly: there were a few farm vehicles on the rather bumpy track. The land you pass through is owned by two families. First you are on West Glen Almond Estate owned by the Montgomery family, then you enter land owned by the Whittaker family. The factor for the Montgomery Estate assured me in 2005 that the track surface was being improved following rain storms the previous year. He also informed me that there was an electrically operated gate for stock control at the Sma' Glen end. Fortunately, the switch is car-driver height and so is suitable for us too.

The landscape is open and gives one the feeling of remoteness. There are tempting tracks winding off into the hills but these, I regret, were for my walking days. Nevertheless, ambling along the wide but bumpy track in showery weather reminded me of yesteryear when I would plod on through rain and mire way up into the remoter hills of the Cairngorms.

The sheep, indifferent to light rain, were their usual grazing selves and the birds made occasional chirps when I ventured too close to their nests. The track follows the River Almond and occasionally is near enough for you to appreciate its babbling. There are two sturdy wooden bridges crossing tributaries to the River Almond. Nearing Auchnafree there are more signs of life but nothing to fear unless barking dogs or cantering horses cause you alarm.

This is a good track for those who seek the solitude of a Scottish Glen.

FURTHER INFORMATION

Perth and Kinross Ranger Service: 01738 475393
Access Officer: 01738 475332

FACT FILE

Map	Ordnance Survey Landranger Sheet 52
Start and Finish	P on A822 NN 889314 / NN 813333
Parking	Small road side P on A822; Auchnafree
Toilets	Centre of Crieff W/C (R) radar
Distance	5 miles / 8 km one way
Landscape	Hillside views

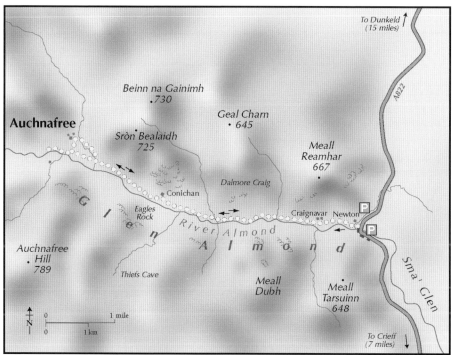

A dreich day in Glen Almond

From Taylor Car Park, go over the bridge and take first left down a steep path to the river. The path then runs alongside the river but is very rutted and full of potholes. Unfortunately, ½ mile further on the path ends in a gated barrier and beyond that the path is accessible by foot only. The local Ranger Service is hoping to access funds to rebuild the path in the next five years.

However, another route can be taken. Do not turn sharp left after the bridge from Taylor Car Park but take the first road left, through the housing estate, and on to the 'wide chicane' (see map). This can be done by car or in your wheelchair. As parking is restricted at the wide chicane, for more than one car it is advisable to use Taylor Car Park.

From the wide chicane the path again leads towards the river and after 300 yards a steep, short but wide, track of 20 yards has to be negotiated. Once by the river, however, a beautiful woodland path runs for 2 miles along the bank of the river before turning back on itself to return, still on a blue route. There is also the choice of a challenging route, through a wide self-closing gate to climb a steep hill on a rough path and the view from the top is lovely. The descent down the other side is equally challenging.

FURTHER INFORMATION

Perth & Kinross Ranger Service: 01768 475393
Access Officer 01738 475332

FACT FILE

Map	Ordnance Survey Landranger Sheets 52
Start and Finish	Taylor Car Park, Crieff (NN 857221)
Parking	Taylor Car Park
Toilets	Centre of Crieff W/C (R) radar
Distance	Blue: 3 miles / 5 km: Red: 4 miles / 6.5 km circular
Landscape	Woodland / river

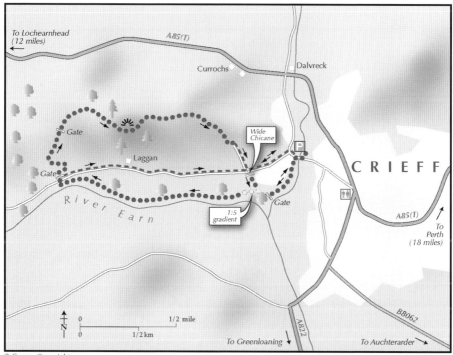

To Lochearnhead
(12 miles)

A85(T)

Currochs

Dalvreck

Gate

Laggan

Wide
Chicane

P

C R I E F F

Gate

River Earn

Gate

1:5
gradient

A85(T)

To
Perth
(18 miles)

N

0   1/2 mile

0   1/2 km

To Greenloaning

B8062

To Auchterarder

© Crown Copyright

By the River Earn

30   Glendevon

Perth & Kinross

Glendevon reservoirs were first suggested to me by a hillwalking friend who thought that rambling here would give me the feeling of open space while being reasonably accessible by wheels. She was right.

This is not an easy walk to find but if you can get yourself to Dollar on the A91 then follow this road east and shortly after Yetts o' Muckhart and before a bridge with sharp bends, turn left on to the A823. Continue for 4 miles until you find a sharp turn off to a small car park on your left.

My friend and I parked here, unloaded the scooter and slowly climbed the long, gentle gradient up into the Ochil Hills. This is an access road to the Glendevon reservoirs and we shortly came across a gate which fortunately allowed pedestrians, including wheelchairs, around the side. Climbing on, we soon passed the lower reservoir with fishermen's cars parked on the roadside.

As we climbed higher and further into the hills that wonderful feeling of getting away from it all grew and grew within me. I looked over at the hills and wondered yet again at the magnificence of nature. After a short time we reached our goal, the top dam, and had our picnic. There were not many trees and we had an unrestricted view. Our only companions were the sheep.

This is another good track for those who seek the solitude of a Scottish Glen.

FURTHER INFORMATION

Perth and Kinross Ranger Service: 01738 475393
Access Officer: 01738 475332

FACT FILE	
Map	Ordnance Survey Landranger Sheet 58
Start and Finish	Car Park on A823 (NN 949052 / NN 939043)
Parking	Parking for 6-8 cars
Toilets	Pub at Tormaukin (narrow door); Blackford Distillery W/C
Distance	6 miles / 9.5 km return
Landscape	Hillside views

WALKING ON WHEELS

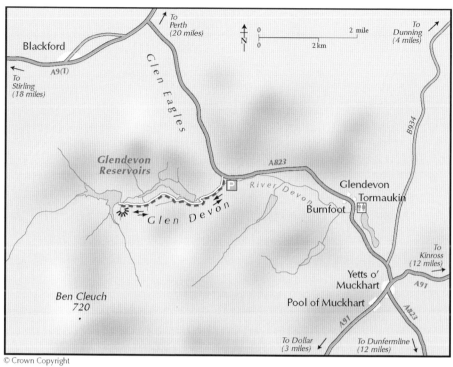

Lower Glendevon Reservoir

FIFE

Despite its relatively small size, Fife has much to offer, with its rich variety of landscapes. The scenery ranges from the high lonely moors of the Lomond and Cleish hills through to the popular coastal habitats of dunes, award winning beaches, cliffs and rocky shores.

In addition, we are fortunate in Fife to have outstanding historic landscapes, such as the picturesque East Neuk fishing villages and the ancient capital of Scotland in Dunfermline. But this is not to ignore the active landscapes, left to us as a legacy of Fife's great industrial history, with the effects of coal and lime extraction, salt manufacture, fishing and agriculture.

So, Fife has something for everyone, from the dedicated wildlife watcher to the student of history and industrial and social archaeology to the person who simply wants to enjoy the outdoors.

This section brings together 10 walks within Fife that give visitors with reduced mobility the chance to catch a glimpse of what's on offer.

For general enquiries about outdoor access or for reporting outdoor access issues in Fife, please contact the Access Officer on 01592 414141, email fife.countryside@fife.gov.uk, or visit: www.fife.gov.uk.

Fife

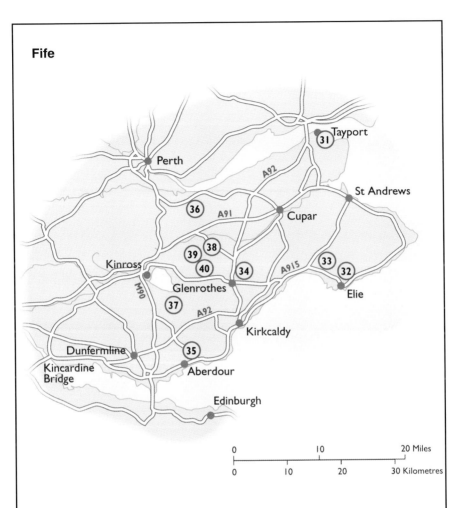

Trail Number	Name	Distance (Miles/Km)
31	Tay Bridge to Tayport & Tentsmuir	2 & 5 / 3 & 8
32	Elie & Shell Bay	3/5
33	Lower Largo & Lundin Links	2/3
34	Balbirnie Park	2/3
35	Aberdour to Burntisland	3/5
36	Pitmedden Forest	3 & 4 / 5 & 6
37	Lochore Meadows Country Park	Various 2 - 4 / 3-6
38	Falkland Estate	Various 1-10 / 1.5-16
39	Lomond Hills	4/6
40	Lomond Hills Reservoirs	2/3

31 Tay Bridge to Tentsmuir

Tay Bridge to Tayport: The official car park for the Fife Coastal Path is 32 steps above the shore line where the Fife Coastal Path begins! However, there are at least two drop-off areas within 50 yards. For 2 miles the path is tarmac and flat with glorious views across the Firth of Tay. Stop at the lighthouse where two benches offer a welcome rest for your walking companions. On entering Tayport there is an official, grassy car park which will take from 6 to 8 cars. Unfortunately, the path deteriorates as far as wheels are concerned and a countryside scooter is recommended for the next 50 yards. After this short challenge the path improves again and takes you along a beautiful, coast-hugging 50 yards, ending at the harbour (see photo). The Fife Coastal Path then takes you through Tayport, including a caravan site, to the start of the second, more challenging trail through Tentsmuir.

Tayport to Tentsmuir: Once you start on the trail through Tentsmuir you are committed to 5 miles of forest track which, after an initial challenge, gets easier. Or you can start at Tentsmuir car park where the track is compact and smooth. Explore for as long as you want and then return whenever you want. On my visit in 2004 we were able to watch the seals which were gathering near the beach in their dozens. But be careful if venturing towards the sea because your wheels will not grip on the sandy surfaces.

Unfortunately, the chicane to the forest at Tayport is only suitable for wheelchairs. If you are visiting on a scooter you are requested to contact the Forestry Commission Ranger in advance to open the locked gate.

FURTHER INFORMATION

Forestry Commission Scotland: 01350 727284. Ranger 07713 053591 (weekends 07810 055787)
www.fifecoastalpath.com

FACT FILE

Map	Ordnance Survey Landranger Sheet 58 & 59
Start and Finish	Tay Bridge (NO 428288), Tayport (NO 498242)
Parking	East of Tayport; Tentsmuir Forest car park
Toilets	Tay Bridge W/C (R) radar; Tayport Harbour W/C (R) radar; Tentsmuir car park W/C (summer only)
Distance	2 miles / 3 km and 5 miles / 8 km or 7 miles / 11 km circular
Landscape	Estuary / coastal path / forest

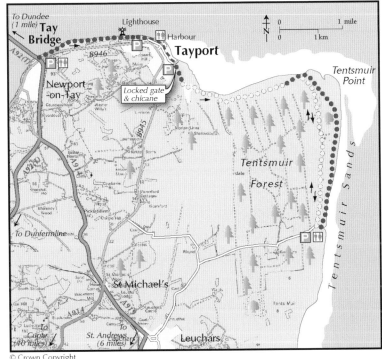

Tayport Harbour

32   Elie & Shell Bay

Take the A917 to the East Neuk of Fife. One mile before Elie a right turn can be taken either by car or in your scooter towards Shell Bay. Here you will find a caravan park where the manager might allow you to use the facilities which are fully accessible. The access around the caravan park is good and leads on the west to a sandy promontory with beautiful views over the Forth. On the east a rutted farm track climbs up and affords a spectacular view of Elie Bay. If you left your car on the A917 you then have the option of taking a rutted farm track heading west for another ½ mile. Elie is a beautiful seaside resort.

Elie Beach, a mile of golden sands, has maintained the high standard recognised by an EnCams award in 2002 for the 'Most Improved Beach Management in the UK'. It is also affectionately known as Ruby Bay because of the famous 'ruby' sometimes washed up on the shore. In summer the harbour is busy with a variety of watersport activities which are fun to watch but parking can be difficult.

You could also take the Fife Coastal Path from the Fife Council car park and head east towards Pittenweem. A path will take you past Elie Ness and offers a magnificent viewpoint.

FURTHER INFORMATION

Fife Countryside Ranger Service: 01592 741212 fife.countryside@fife.gov.uk
www.fifecoastalpath.com

FACT FILE

Map	Ordnance Survey Landranger Sheet 59
Start and Finish	Shell Bay Caravan Park (NO 464004)
	Elie Harbour (NO 492995)
Parking	Shell Bay; Elie Harbour / East Elie Fife Council: 6ft / 1.7m high barrier
Toilets	Shell Bay W/C; Elie W/C (R); East Elie P&T W/C (L)
Distance	Both walks are approx. 3 miles / 5 km circular
Landscapes	Seascapes

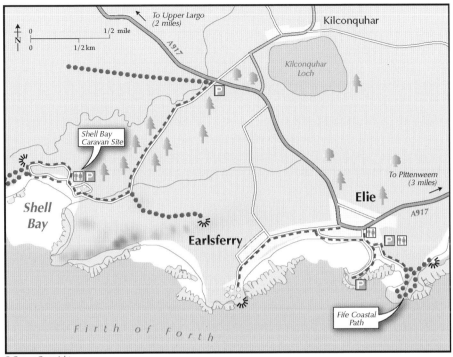

Breaking waves at Shell Bay

33 Lower Largo & Lundin Links

Although I now live in Fife, I was brought up in Glasgow. In the 1960s there was a great exodus of Glaswegians every summer to the beautiful shores of the Forth. My family came every year to Lundin Links or Lower Largo and I have very fond memories of these seaside towns. Although I was very young at the time, being the youngest in my family, we often went for walks and it was with great delight that I returned to old haunts to audit them for disabled rambling.

There are many walks of various length and difficulty in this relatively small area. Some are within the villages themselves and these are depicted by the broken lines, blue and yellow, indicating that the pavements are not always wheelchair friendly. There are three countryside trails: to the west through the golf courses; to the north along a forest trail to Keil's Den; to the east from the old railway line towards Upper Largo. You could spend a whole day enjoying the sea air and experiencing a links golf course, a small busy harbour, a yachting marina, beach views, a challenging countryside trail (red) and/or a beautiful forest trail leading to a riverside picnic area.

Parking is reasonable throughout the villages with designated parking shown on the map. Unfortunately, disabled toilet facilities are not good. You have to search the hotels, and be prepared to purchase sustenance to find a fully accessible toilet. Most of the hotels offer what in their opinion is an accessible toilet but in my opinion is not fully, wheelchair accessible.

FURTHER INFORMATION

Fife Countryside Ranger Service: Tel. 01592 741212
fife.countryside@fife.gov.uk
www.fifecoastalpath.com

FACT FILE

Map	Ordnance Survey Landranger Sheet 59
Start Points	Keil's Den (NO 417035)
	Harbour (NO 417025)
Parking	2 Public car parks in Lower Largo; street parking
Toilets	Very poor choice. Only public toilet is walk in
Distance	2 miles / 3 km linear through villages
	1 mile / 1.5 to Keil's Den from Harbour
Landscape	Seascape or forest track

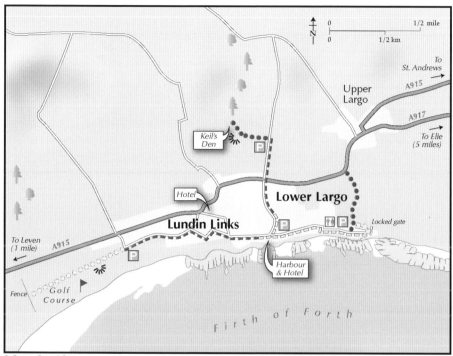

© Crown Copyright

Keil's Den

34 Balbirnie Park

Fife

We have lived in Markinch for twenty-seven years. Balbirnie Park is on our doorstep and has given me, my husband and four children many hours of recreation in a beautiful setting. When I became a wheelchair and scooter user I was delighted to find that Balbirnie Park was still accessible. There are many miles of well-surfaced, stable paths and the majority are reasonably flat. However, the park includes a steep hill: it has good paths but a strong scooter and stout resolve is necessary to reach the top.

The park is well-known for its magnificent display of rhododendrons in the spring and trees which have come from South America. The Stone Circle is believed to be Stone Age and is well worth a visit. The old stable block is currently used as a craft centre where merchandise can be bought most days. Unfortunately, the jeweller and the picture gallery are upstairs.

There are three car parks: a public one at the entrance and the other two are private. Of these, one is at the golf clubhouse and the other belongs to Balbirnie House Hotel. The only toilets are within the private golf clubhouse and hotel and they are both wheelchair (not scooter) accessible. The access to the golf clubhouse is by a long, narrow ramped entrance to the restaurant Fire Exit but once in the clubhouse the view of the 18th green is spectacular for anybody interested in golf. Unfortunately, admission is only possible by arrangement or with a club member.

FURTHER INFORMATION

Amenities and history of Balbirnie Park: www.fifedirect.org.uk
Fife Countryside Ranger Service: 01592 741212 fife.countryside@fife.gov.uk.

FACT FILE

Map	Ordnance Survey Landranger Sheet 59
Start and Finish	Car Park at NO 293018
Parking	Entrance at Markinch from the B9130
Toilets	Private only: Balbirnie House Hotel W/C (R); Golf Club W/C (L)
Distance	2 miles / 3 km circular; many miles of other paths
Landscape	Woodland / golf course / small burn / Stone Age Circle

96 WALKING ON WHEELS

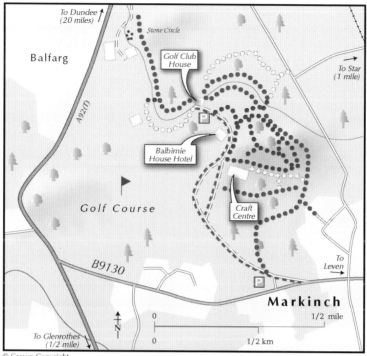

Balfarg

To Dundee
(20 miles)

Stone Circle

Golf Club
House

To Star
(1 mile)

A92(T)

P

Balbirnie
House Hotel

Golf Course

Craft
Centre

B9130

To
Leven

P

Markinch

N

0   1/2 mile

0   1/2 km

To Glenrothes
(1/2 mile)

Burn in Balbirnie Park

35 Aberdour to Burntisland

My fellow rambler, James Page, is enthusiastic about environmental improvements on the Fife Coastal Path between Aberdour and Burntisland: 'The water is beautifully clear, and reminded me of the waters off the west coast when I first saw them back in the 1970s, which were then a sharp contrast to the Forth Estuary, but with which it could now stand comparison. Also gorse and bluebells were in flower, and a blackbird sang his heart out for us on a tree by the water's edge. And there were a couple of seals with a baby, basking on some rocks. Who needs to go abroad looking for Nirvana: it's in your own back yard.'

I have visited this path twice. On the first occasion I went in my scooter and I was glad of it as the path was quite tricky due to the wet conditions resulting in a very muddy path. The second visit I made in my electric wheelchair. I got off the train at Aberdour, followed the path through the castle and then detoured from the Fife Coastal Path to access Silversands Bay by road. A further mile along the path there is a very steep short section which is challenging because of exposed tree roots on top of a steep slope. The ranger assured me they had considered felling the offending tree but it was thought too precious to be removed. I would therefore advise using a countryside scooter with high clearance or having a strong able-bodied helper with you.

Silversands Bay is a beautiful cove much visited by young families. There are several car parks and a small café serves food both indoors and on the terrace.

FURTHER INFORMATION

Fife Countryside Ranger Service: 01592 741212 fife.countryside@fife.gov.uk
www.fifecoastalpath.com

FACT FILE

Map	Ordnance Survey Landranger Sheet 65 & 66
Start	Aberdour (NT 191854)
Finish	Burntisland (NT 232856)
Parking	Silversands Bay £1; Lower Car Park restricted until 5 p.m. but disabled access is free
Toilets	Silversands Bay W/C accessible (R&L) April to Sept; Disabled toilet next to Swell café (enter from shore side)
Distance	3 miles / 5 km one way
Landscape	Coastal

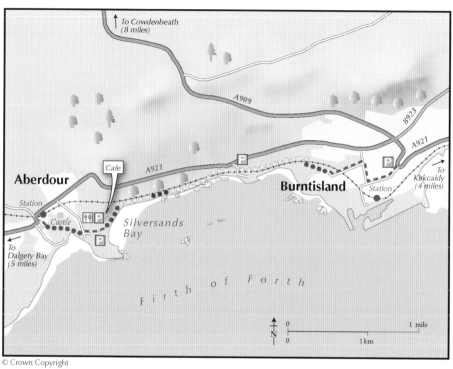

Evening light at Aberdour Beach

36   Pitmedden Forest

My husband recommended this forest trail but warned me that some paths were very steep. So avoiding the really steep routes, off we set. The forest is managed by Forestry Commission Scotland (FCS), Tay District, and is well signposted for cyclists. Consequently, it is reasonably well maintained and any path problems should be reported to FCS (see below).

Although a small forest by FCS standards, it gives the walker the accustomed sounds, smells and atmosphere associated with forests everywhere in Scotland: that aroma of pine wood and natural mulch with the sound of swaying branches all around. Being in the east and near the sea, the Firth of Tay, the trees are not of the magnificent splendour you find in the west but nevertheless that timeless, meditative ambience is definitely present.

There are parking places at either end of the forest – in the west on the minor road between Strathmiglo and Abernethy and in the east not far from Falkland, so it is well placed. As you can see from the map, trails of various grades are available and all in all it is a pleasant place to visit.

We saw deer, not running wild but farmed and in a field to the west of the forest. I find there is something very ancient and majestic about deer, much more so than the lowly cow. I have not been to Reedie Hill Farm but I believe venison is on sale there.

FURTHER INFORMATION

Fife Countryside Ranger Service: 01592 741212 fife.countryside@fife.gov.uk
Forestry Commission Scotland: 01350 727284. Ranger: 07713 053591
(weekends 07810 055787)

FACT FILE	
Map	Ordnance Survey Landranger Sheet 58
Start and Finish	Car Park at NO 222130 / NO 198141
Parking	East and west end of forest
Toilets	Falkland town centre small W/C (R)
Distance	3 miles / 5 km linear (P to P); 4 miles / 6.5 km circular from east P
Landscape	Forest

WALKING ON WHEELS

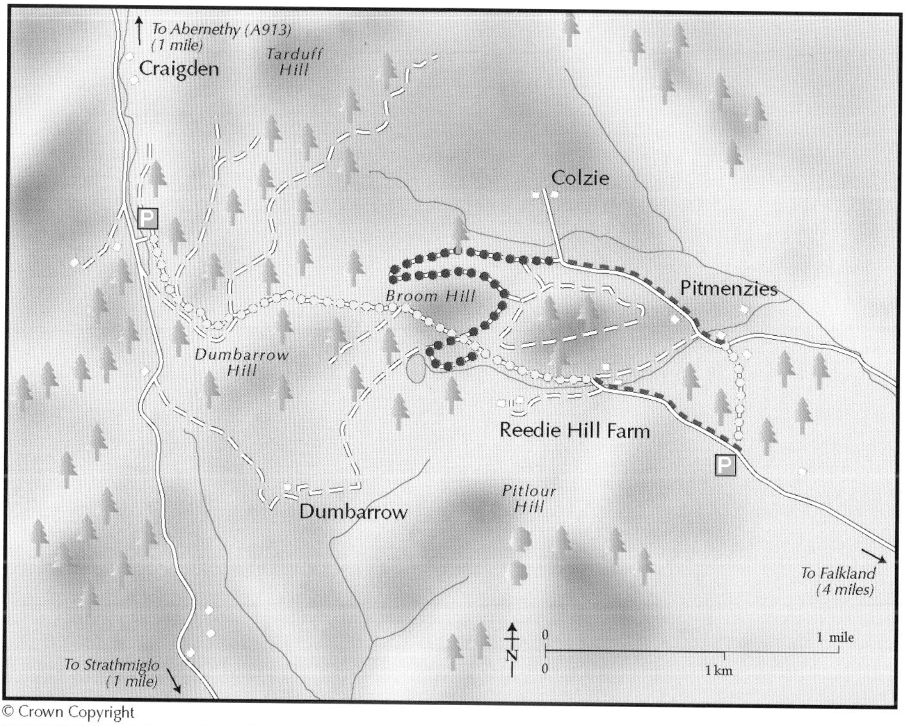
To Abernethy (A913)
(1 mile)
Craigden
Tarduff
Hill
Colzie
Broom Hill
Pitmenzies
Dumbarrow
Hill
Reedie Hill Farm
Dumbarrow
Pitlour
Hill
To Falkland
(4 miles)
N
0
1 mile
0
1 km
To Strathmiglo
(1 mile)

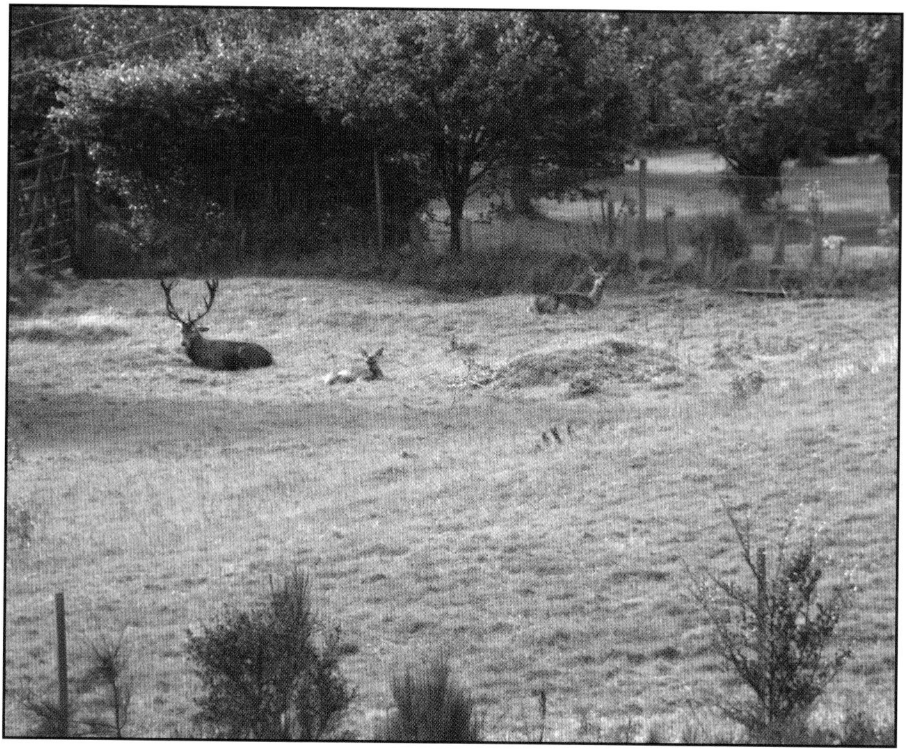

Deer Farm at Pitmedden

37 Lochore Meadows Country Park
Lomond Hills Regional Park, Fife

Lochore Meadows Country Park is within the Lomond Hills Regional Park (see Walks 37, 39 and 40). I have visited the Meadows on many occasions. The land has been reclaimed from a former coal mining site and is full of interest. It is worth picking up information leaflets or asking for a guided tour.

It is easy to spend a day meandering around the several miles of fully accessible paths. It is worth enquiring about other paths not outlined here. Unfortunately, when I have visited, it was not possible to access the south side of the loch but I believe access is planned. The accessible bird hide, on the west side, offers good water fowl viewing.

There are two fully accessible centres: one for the parkland and the other for outdoor facilities. The outdoor education centre has several pieces of equipment suitable for the less mobile, e.g. adapted cycles, a wheelie boat for fishing and accessible sailing boats. James Page wrote of his sailing experience here: 'I got in this sailing boat along with three other rookies and a girl who knew what to do. Our instructions were basic: pull on the rope and duck when we turn. As the wind gave us quite a bit of speed we turned frequently, and covered most of the loch in what seemed like no time at all.'

In order to prevent the Pit Road (a quiet rural road) becoming a through route the Council, unfortunately, has had to install locked gates in two places. However, keys are available on loan from the Park Centre which is open from 9 a.m. to 5 p.m. every day.

FURTHER INFORMATION

Fife Countryside Ranger Service: 01592 741212 fife.countryside@fife.gov.uk
Lochore Meadows: Tel 01592 414300 info@lochore-meadows.co.uk
www.lochore-meadows.co.uk

FACT FILE	
Map	Ordnance Survey Landranger Sheet 59
Start and Finish	Car Park at NT 160960
Parking	Park Centre (10 designated Disabled bays); Outdoor Education Centre (4 designated Disabled bays)
Toilets	Park Centre W/C (R); Outdoor Education Centre W/C (L)
Distance	Various: 2 miles / 3 km to 4 miles / 6.5 km circular
Landscape	Rolling hills / freshwater fowl / water sports / flora.

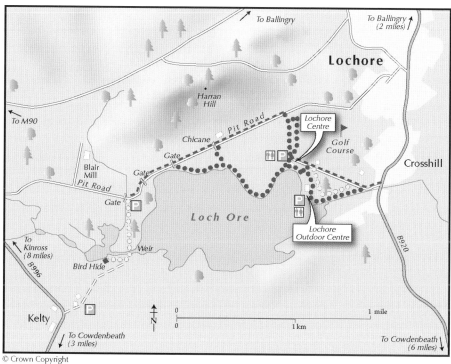

Lochore Meadows

38   Falkland Estate

I have many memories, all of them good, of rambling around the Falkland Estate which is also part of the Lomond Hills Regional Park. The estate land is used for farming, forestry and recreation. Flora and fauna are numerous and delightful but it is the peace and tranquility, enhanced by the natural burns and numerous bridges, that make it so attractive.

The Falkland Heritage Trust has reinstated much of the path network to the original design in the days of our hunting kings. Unfortunately, due to gradients, land formation and stock control not every path has been made fully accessible. However, it is possible for all types of wheelchair and scooter users to spend a whole day rambling around the estate. Guided walks are on offer throughout the summer. Leaflets can be obtained from the Falkland Heritage Trust.

There are easier trails nearer to Falkland itself, while further west there are harder routes which I have shown in red, including the route to the fine viewpoint on Black Hill and another which visits a pretty waterfall.

It would be hard not to visit Falkland, a Best Kept Village award winner, and not visit the magnificent Falkland Palace Gardens (National Trust for Scotland property). Unfortunately, the Palace itself is not accessible for wheelchairs. This has been a royal residence since 1460, a place where the early Stuart kings came to work, rest, and play 'real' tennis.

FURTHER INFORMATION

Falkland Heritage Trust: 01337 858838 admin@falklandht.org.uk
Fife Countryside Ranger Service: fife.countryside@fife.gov.uk
www.fifecoastalpath.com

FACT FILE	
Map	Ordnance Survey Landranger Sheet 58 & 59
Start and Finish	Duck pond (NO 246074)
Parking	Falkland & Falkland Estate
Toilets	Falkland Town Centre, small W/C (R); Pillars of Hercules, small W/C (L)
Distance	Circular: 1 mile / 1.5 km up to 10 miles / 16 km
Landscape	Woodland / hillside / Palace Gardens

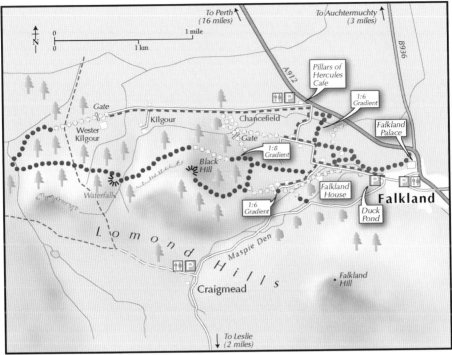

Bridge in Lower Maspie Den

39 Lomond Hills

It is possible to start your ramble on to the Lomond Hills from Falkland by taking the B936 and climbing the steep, windy road to Craigmead car park. Or you can meander through Falkland Estate to join this road half way there. Or you can simply park at Craigmead to start your long, slow climb on to either West Lomond or Falkland Hill. I say 'slow' because that is the best way to appreciate these hills and the views they offer towards and beyond both the Forth & Tay Estuaries.

Access from Craigmead to West Lomond is across sheep grids which did not challenge my scooter wheels but might be difficult for smaller wheels. The gates to Falkland Hill, on the other hand, require a key from the Lomond Hills Regional Park rangers at Pitcairn. There is a chicane at the Craigmead entrance which the larger scooter might struggle to get through.

Once on the hillside there is a real 'away from it all' feeling. The skies are high and the views long, that is, in good weather. But whenever you go remember to wrap up well or take appropriate warm clothing as it is quite high and the weather can change quite suddenly.

West Lomond is the highest point in the whole of Fife, at 522 metres (1712 feet), so it is not surprising that it commands an extensive view. I'm told that from East Lomond (424m / 1390ft, also called Falkland Hill) you can look down at the old village spread below you.

FURTHER INFORMATION

fife.countryside@fife.gov.uk
Pitcairn Centre: 01592 741212 fife.countryside@fife.gov.uk
www.fifedirect.org.uk; www.fifecoastalpath.com

FACT FILE

Map	Ordnance Survey Landranger Sheet 58 & 59
Start and Finish	Craigmead (NO 227062)
Parking	Craigmead
Toilets	Craigmead car park W/C (L), open daylight hours
Distance	Linear: 4 miles / 6.5 km x 2 walks
Landscape	Open hills with views over Tay and Forth Estuaries

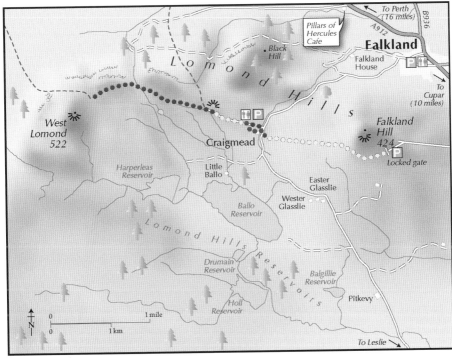

New path to West Lomond

40 Lomond Hills Reservoirs

I am very fortunate in having such a variety of walks on wheels in my neighbourhood. Within ten minutes by car I can be out and about in the Lomond Hills Regional Park. I can even access it directly by scooter by going through Glenrothes, then north to Pitcairn. Here I have a choice of a circular path around Coul Reservoir or linear/return on to the hillside via the horse track.

If, however, you seek a longer route with more dramatic views of the Forth and, indeed, of the Lomond Hills, then I recommend a gentle climb up past Holl, Drumain, Ballo and Harperleas Reservoirs. The tracks are good enough for a manual wheelchair but it would be quite a haul self-propelling or being pushed. I have, therefore, suggested, by marking the route yellow on the map, that some battery power is advisable. Despite being so close to civilisation there is a feeling of remote nature as soon as you hit the Lomond Hills. Even the farmed animals, highland cows and sheep, do not intrude but blend in with their wild companions, deer and water fowl, which were quick to move in to new habitat created by man-made lochs. The Fife Countryside Rangers have many information leaflets from 'Shared Access' and 'Baked, Buckled & Frozen' to 'Exploring the Lomond Hills' available from Pitcairn Centre.

As the hills are very exposed, be sure to take stout rainwear with you.

FURTHER INFORMATION

Falkland Heritage Trust: 01337 858838
Fife Countryside Ranger Service: fife.countryside@fife.gov.uk
Pitcairn Centre: 01592 741212 fife.countryside@fife.gov.uk
www.fifedirect.org.uk; www.fifecoastalpath.com

FACT FILE

Map	Ordnance Survey Landranger Sheets 58 & 59
Start and Finish	Pitcairn (Sheet 58: NO 225034 / NO 202054)
	Holl (Sheet 59: NO 273010 / NO 262034)
Parking	Glenrothes; Pitcairn (10 hard core); Holl (8 tarmac)
Toilets	Glenrothes Town Centre W/C (R) radar
Distance	Holl: 4 miles / 6.5 km linear return
	Pitcairn: 2 miles / 3 km circular
Landscape	Open hills with views over Forth Estuary

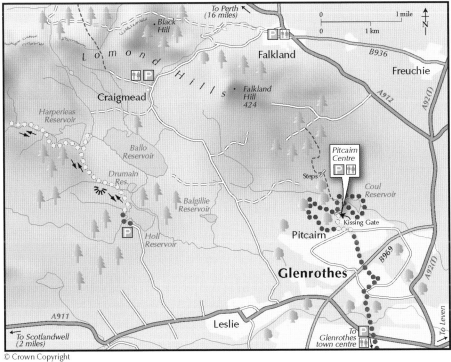

Lomond Hills Reservoirs

CENTRAL SCOTLAND

S cotland's Central Belt has a surprising amount to offer the walker, with plenty of variety and a good mix of landscape.

Two of the walks follow sections of the canal system, recently upgraded as part of the large-scale Millennium Link project. Canal towpaths are generally flat and parts have good views too, and one walk visits the amazing Falkirk Wheel, the world's largest boat lift. Information available from British Waterways will lead you to many other canal walks.

There are several fine Country Parks in the region, and we visit one of them, Almondell. This park, deep in the industrial hinterland of West Lothian, is based around the valley of the River Almond, and another fine river, the Water of Leith, is also included. The Water of Leith has a well-graded path following almost its entire length from the Pentland Hills down to the Firth of Forth at Leith, Edinburgh's port.

The section included here runs from Balerno to Slateford and includes several wooded sections and even a short tunnel, formerly part of a railway line.

Another section of Edinburgh's shoreline is followed at Portobello, once a fashionable resort, and the final walk takes us deep into the Pentland Hills south of Edinburgh, walking beside two beautiful reservoirs.

These six walks offer a tempting sample of Central Scotland's many attractions and you are sure to enjoy them all.

For general enquiries about outdoor access or for reporting outdoor access issues, please contact the relevant Access Officer for the trail: Glasgow 0141 287 8585; Falkirk 01324 504721; West Lothian 01506 775249 and Edinburgh 0131 529 7883.

Central Scotland

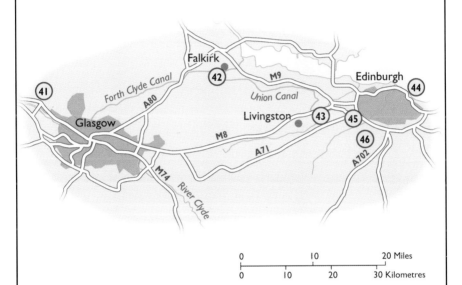

Trail Number	Name	Distance (Miles/Km)
41	Forth & Clyde Canal: Bowling to Glasgow	12/19
42	Falkirk Wheel	4-10 / 6-16
43	Almondell Country Park	2/3
44	Portobello	1/1.5
45	Water of Leith	3/5
46	Pentland Hills Reservoirs	4/6

41 Bowling to Glasgow

Much has been written on the history and refurbishment of one of Scotland's transport heritages – the Forth & Clyde (F&C) Canal. A recent publication from British Waterways called *Exploring Scotland's Lowland Canals and the Millennium Link* is worthy of its £1 purchase price. The section of canal, the last to be built, which links the City of Glasgow with the Clyde Estuary was finished in 1790.

On my visit in November 2004 I found that 95% of the towpath was level and of reasonable surface. There are 13 locks and occasionally the gradient, although short, could be as steep as 1:9. Puddles were sometimes deep and could be muddy, especially at some of the path's 25 chicanes. All chicanes are now wide enough for scooter access.

This 12-mile stretch of the canal offers both urban and rural vistas. From the west you can scan the wide Clyde Estuary and draw in breath while under the awesome Erskine Bridge which towers above. You may wish to stop to shop at Clydebank or have a drink at Lock 27 pub at Temple. The restored Maryhill Locks are another highlight, and on this stretch you may well see swans and other wildlife. South of Firhill (see map) and if the weather is fair you will enjoy a breathtaking view of much of Glasgow, including the impressive University of Glasgow.

FURTHER INFORMATION

British Waterways HQ: Canal House, 1 Applecross St., Glasgow G4 9SP
0141 354 7501, www.waterscape.com
Towpath enquiries: 01324 671217
Glasgow Access Officer: 0141 287 8585

FACT FILE	
Map	Ordnance Survey Landranger Sheet 64
Start and Finish	Bowling (NS 451735); Spiers Wharf (NS 584672)
Parking	Bowling Basin, BWS HQ and on road along the route
Toilets	BWS at Temple W/C (L) most days
Distance	12 miles / 19 km one way
Landscape	Clyde estuary / rural canal scenes / cityscapes.

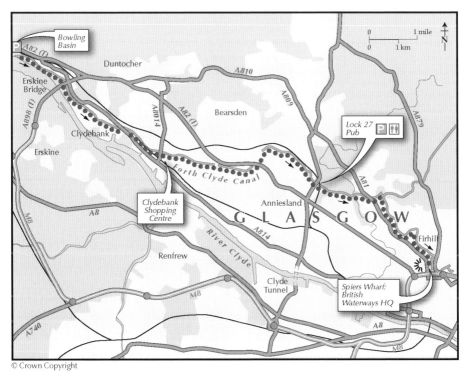

© Crown Copyright

Typical canal towpath

42 Falkirk Wheel

The Falkirk Wheel is now one of Scotland's most visited attractions. It offers a good day out for the whole family and now has wheelchair accessible boats for the Wheel itself. Perhaps you prefer to be al fresco in which case there is a choice of towpath wheelchair rambling in three directions. The numerous chicanes installed to bar motor cyclists have been widened and are no longer a barrier to scooters.

On the Forth & Clyde Canal set off west and eventually you will reach Bowling 33 miles away to the west of Glasgow (see map 41). But I suggest you get someone to meet you at Auchinstarry, a mere 10 miles away. Or set off east through Falkirk to Carron Lock and the Firth of Forth, 4 miles away. Or climb up to the Union Canal and set off towards Edinburgh and take the double challenge of the Falkirk Tunnel and Avon Aqueduct and be rewarded with views of Linlithgow Palace, 11 miles away. With all of these routes puddles can be deep and can be muddy, especially at chicanes.

For thrills and views it has to be the Linlithgow trail. If setting off from the Falkirk Wheel in a manual wheelchair you will need a strong pusher for the short but steep path to the upper level. The Falkirk Tunnel is about half a mile long, full of puddles and poorly lit. So I would recommend scooters only. The Avon aqueduct is equally challenging and although I crossed it in my electric wheelchair I would advise a scooter. The views are spectacular and at one point you are on a level with the birds at the top of 30 ft tall trees. Linlithgow is a beautiful old town with paths around the loch negotiable by scooter.

FURTHER INFORMATION

British Waterways HQ: 0141 354 7501
The Falkirk Wheel: 08700 500 208 www.thefalkirkwheel.co.uk
Towpath enquiries: 01324 671217
Access Officer: Falkirk Wheel 01324 504721; West Lothian 01506 775249

FACT FILE	
Map	Ordnance Survey Landranger Sheet 65
Start and Finish	Falkirk Wheel (NS 885796)
Parking	Falkirk Wheel; Linlithgow; Carron Basin
Toilets	Falkirk Wheel W/C (R); Carron Basin BW manned W/C (L); Auchinstarry Basin W/C
Distance	10 miles / 16 km; 4 miles / 6.5 km; 11 miles / 17.5 km
Landscape	Waterscape / canal / townscape

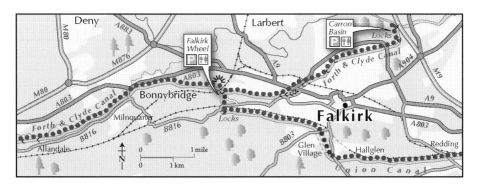

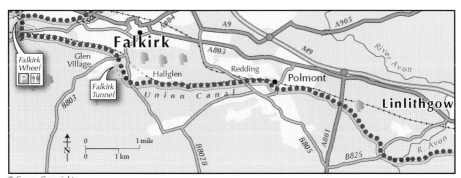

Visitors' boat at the Falkland Wheel

43 Almondell & Calderwood Country Park
Livingston

This is not the easiest park to find despite its good signposting. It is possibly best to approach it from the north, either from the M8, turning off south at junction 3 towards Livingston, or, as we did, turn off from Broxburn (signposted on the A89) on to a minor road. This will take you directly to Almondell & Calderwood Country Park. The park, which is on land formerly owned by the Erskine family, Earls of Buchan, was opened in 1981. It is based on the valley of the River Almond and, as well as the extensive path network, its many attractions include a curious 'astronomical pillar', a lovely old bridge designed by the painter Alexander Nasmyth, and a dramatic railway viaduct.

When you arrive you will find a haven of peace and tranquillity right on the edges of manufacturing Scotland. Minutes away is Livingston, one of Scotland's New Towns. But here you could be in the heart of rural bliss. The trees are grand and the River Almond is a wee, meandering beauty. Natural flora and fauna are all around and the smell of wild garlic is intoxicating. I was very lucky to spy a heron the first year I visited. It swooped past me flapping loudly as it flew close to the top of the water looking for fish.

There is a choice of routes. You can stick to the tarmacadam road or venture along the paths. However, at the present time, if you visit in a wheelchair with small front wheels you may find the entrances and exits both on to the paths and the bridges along these routes quite challenging.

FURTHER INFORMATION

Almondell & Calderwood Country Park, Visitor Centre: 01506 882254
almondell&calderwood@westlothian.gov.uk
Access Officer: 01506 775249

FACT FILE

Map	Ordnance Survey Landranger Sheet 65
Start and Finish	Visitor Centre NT 091692
Parking	Access for Disabled to Lower Car Park through barrier
Toilets	Visitor Centre W/C (L&R); Park Toilet (Winter 10–4 p.m. Summer 9–5 p.m. Closed lunch)
Distance	2 miles / 3 km – 6 miles / 9.5 km
Landscape	Riverside / woodland

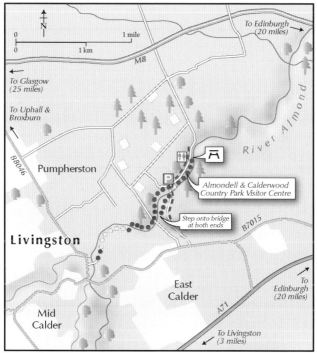

© Crown Copyright

Almondell path and viaduct

44 Portobello

If you want a bracing ride along a beautiful, old seafront promenade then Portobello is the place to go. Until the middle of the 18th century, Portobello remained an area of barren heath beside the Firth of Forth, about 5 miles to the east of Edinburgh. The first house was built by George Hamilton in 1755 (and demolished in 1862). It was named Portobello House, after Puerto Bello on the Isthmus of Panama where Hamilton survived a naval battle. Some elegant houses were added between 1770 and 1830.

The promenade can be accessed from either end or from the middle. If arriving from Edinburgh by public transport, take the train from Waverley to Brunstane and head north to the Portobello Leisure Centre and from here you can head east or west. Going along the Prom you have the opportunity to visualise the old town as it might have been over 100 years ago. The first bathing machines were reported at Portobello in 1795, and a pier with a camera obscura was built in 1871. There was an open air Art Deco swimming pool with high boards and generating 3 ft high waves which has now been demolished. Portobello indoor bowls stands in its place. The west end is more industrial. A ferry used to traverse the Forth from Portobello and it is easy to imagine boarding the boat here.

At this point you can return via the town of Portobello along the A199 or retrace your steps along the promenade and head east towards Musselburgh. Although retracing steps along linear routes may seem boring, the views are so different that it is worth doing. The view of the East Lothian and Fife coast and beyond to the North Sea is quite entrancing.

FURTHER INFORMATION
Access Officer: 0131 529 7883

FACT FILE	
Map	Ordnance Survey Landranger Sheet 66
Start and Finish	Portobello (NT 292757 / NT 328731)
Parking	On road
Toilets	Public (radar key); Indoor Bowls W/C (L); Leisure Centre W/C (R); 28 in / 70 cm lift door
Distance	2 miles / 3 km return
Landscape	Seascape

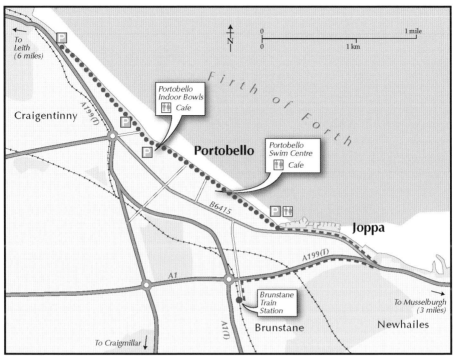

Wheels along the Prom

45 Water of Leith

I was delighted when I was asked by the Edinburgh Council Ranger who works closely with the Water of Leith Conservation Trust to join him on the Water of Leith Walkway to assess it for access from a wheelchair user's point of view. We arranged to meet outside Balerno Community School, together with an Edinburgh friend who also uses an electric wheelchair. We set off down a fairly steep but well-surfaced access path to the Water of Leith Walkway.

There is much to see on this walkway and you should allow yourself time to stop and ponder at the many sites of historical interest along the route. The Water of Leith is designated an Urban Wildlife Site. More than 80 bird species have been recorded here and you might even see a heron or a kingfisher. Foxes, badgers, otters and bats also make their homes along the river. As someone brought up near the Botanic Gardens in Glasgow I have been accustomed to tall trees and paths by rivers in an urban setting. There is something very pleasing about the mix of town and country and, judging by the number of pedestrians and cyclists we met during our visit, obviously I am not the only one who feels this way.

At Craiglockhart those on wheels take a slight diversion, over Lanark Road to join the Union Canal, just west of the Slateford Aqueduct. At this point you can join the canal towpath and go west to Falkirk, or east across Slateford Aqueduct and on a further 2 miles to the new canal basin at Edinburgh Quays. I would recommend a scooter for the aqueduct. A useful book is the guide *The Water of Leith Walkway* available at £2.70 from the Trust's Visitor Centre.

FURTHER INFORMATION

Water of Leith Conservation Trust Centre: 0131 455 7367,
www.waterofleith.org.uk, Access Officer: 0131 529 7883

FACT FILE

Map	Ordnance Survey Landranger Sheet 65 & 66
Start and Finish	Balerno (NT 164669); Slateford (NT 215704)
Parking	Bridge Road, Balerno; Lanark Road, Edinburgh
Toilets	WOL Conservation Trust Visitor Centre W/C (R) 10–4 p.m; Balerno Community School W/C Ladies (L) Gents (R)
Distance	5 miles / 8 km (10 miles / 16 km return)
Landscape	Riverside townscape

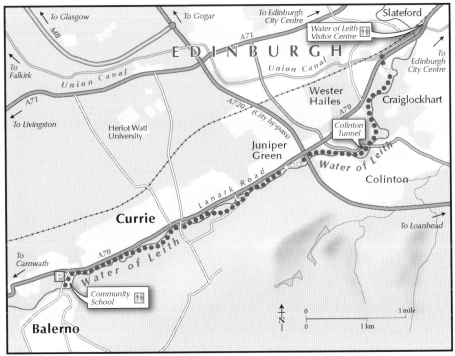

Water of Leith townscape

46   Pentland Reservoirs

This walk was suggested to me by my husband, a keen hill walker, as one he thought I could do easily on my own. He was right. This is a trail completely on tarmac, but the only passing cars are fishermen on their way to Loganlea Trout Fishery. The only difficulties I came across were the cattle grids with side kissing gates which would have been difficult to open had I been unable to get out of my scooter.

For 3 miles I climbed slowly up into the Pentland Hills. I went on a lovely sunny day and there is nothing nicer than the sun glinting on the water, the road dappled in tree shadows and the hills as a backdrop. At the top end I explored a little, but being on my own I did not go far. I hope to return one day to see how far up the track into the Pentland Hills my scooter would take me. As it was, I sat and had my picnic and watched the fishermen gently rowing around a reservoir. (Grid reference NT 19161 car pick-up is possible here.)

On the way back down I stopped to chat to the owner of the Loganlea Trout Fishery. He told me he was hoping to install a launching pad from where one could fish from a wheelchair.

Recently I returned for a short 2-mile ramble and found the radar key lock had been officially 'disabled' giving access for all. I also tested the All Ability track from the car park for ¼ mile through woodland. This runs parallel to the road but please note that there are no passing or turning places.

FURTHER INFORMATION

Loganlea Trout Fishery: 01968 676329
Pentland Hills Ranger Service: 0131 445 3383
Access Officer: 0131 529 7883

FACT FILE

Map	Ordnance Survey Landranger Sheet 66
Start and Finish	Flotterstone (NT 233631)
Parking	Flotterstone Information Centre, 3 Disabled bays
Toilets	Flotterstone Information Centre W/C (L)
Distance	6 miles / 9.5 km return
Landscape	Hills / water

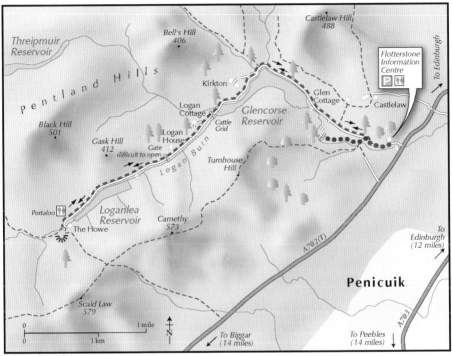

Pentlands Reservoir

DUMFRIES & GALLOWAY

Dumfries and Galloway is Scotland's most southerly region. It offers a quality of life that is second to none.

The region combines the best of a modern society with the legacy of its unique heritage. It has unspoilt scenery, spectacular coastline and contrasting landscapes, with forest and lochs, hills and rolling plains, rugged cliffs and sandy beaches. It has refreshing countryside, bustling market towns, a mild climate and a wealth of history, wildlife and heritage.

It also has a stunning blend of countryside waiting to be discovered, from its magnificent coastlines with views of England, Ireland and the Isle of Man to the rolling hills and crags of the Southern Uplands.

Dumfries and Galloway attracts visitors for a wide range of outdoor activities including water sports on Loch Ken, cycling on the quiet country roads or an off-road challenge. Yet Dumfries and Galloway still retains a natural feel with ample space for all to enjoy. This section brings together 4 walks within Dumfries and Galloway that give visitors with reduced mobility the chance to catch a glimpse of what's on offer.

For general enquiries about outdoor access or for reporting outdoor access issues in Dumfries and Galloway please contact the Access Officer on 01387 260145 or visit www.dumgal.gov.uk/countrysideaccess.

Dumfries & Galloway

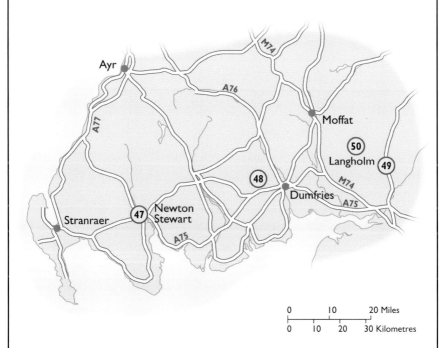

Trail Number	Name	Distance (Miles/Km)
47	Kirroughtree	8/13
48	Glen Kiln	6/10
49	Langholm	3/5
50	Meggat Water	5/8

47 Kirroughtree

Dumfries & Galloway

Kirroughtree is part of the Galloway Forest Park which is managed by Forestry Commission Scotland. It has its own Outdoor Recreation Officer and Visitor Centre Manager who can assist with information and helpful advice.

Dumfries and Galloway is known as the forgotten Scotland and this is sad because it is really very attractive. As a wheelchair user I can understand why it could be neglected: finding an accessible B&B proved difficult. However, I can strongly recommend day visits and, although I did not allow enough time to do it justice, a return visit is high on my list. There are so many places of interest to visit, from gardens to seaside and hillside walks.

Kirroughtree has been developed for visitors. The trails are well mapped and signposted. I have only included trails 4 & 6 on my map as these are the numbers most pertinent for the route I followed. The track we took started and stopped steeply which is why I have graded it red. Apart from these two steep slopes the paths are quite flat although they are still bumpy. The views from the top are not spectacular but they are very pleasant, and there is the usual attraction of being in a mature forest.

FURTHER INFORMATION

Galloway Forest Park: 01671 402420

FACT FILE

Map	Ordnance Survey Landranger Sheet 83
Start and Finish	Kirroughtree Forest (NX 453646)
Parking	Kirroughtree Visitor Centre
Toilets	Kirroughtree Visitor Centre W/C (L)
Distance	6 miles / 9.5 km
Landscape	Woodland

Dumfries & Galloway

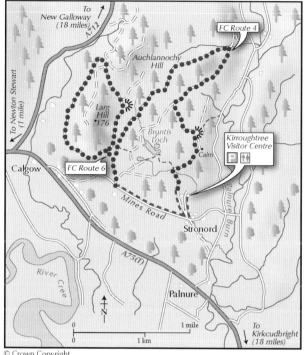

Lush Galloway forest

48 Glenkiln

What a fantastic find. If Dumfries & Galloway is the forgotten Scotland then Glenkiln is its hidden jewel! How amazing to come across Henry Moore and Rodin sculptures out in the countryside. I am not an art connoisseur but the delight in coming upon these sculptures, marked on OS map 84, made me gasp. There they were sharing space with nature, both wild and domestic. Being early summer, the field leading to the sculpture on the red track had calves with their mothers and dad so we followed the Scottish Outdoor Access Code and missed that one out.

The trail was on a very minor single track road and I think we were passed by only two cars the whole morning. There were sheep a-plenty, and with stock come cattle grids. Fortunately, they all had side gates but, unfortunately, at least half were overgrown and we did not even attempt to open them. The grids were reasonably smooth. We parked at the top end of Glenkiln Reservoir, at sculpture 2, headed over our first grid to the sculpture marked 1, then retraced back to the reservoir and followed it to a crossroads where we turned right to sculpture 4. The reservoir had many waterfowl and the tall conifers gave a grand feel to the place.

Having reached the third sculpture, another Henry Moore, I was unable to resist continuing up and over the glen and then just kept going. The farm track to Peartree Hill looked very smooth and although I did not have time to explore I have graded it blue. Continuing down towards the A712 takes you through a lovely deciduous forest. There is a lay-by on the A712 and if you are able to arrange a car pick-up, this makes a good 6-mile linear walk. En route you pass a lochan which seems to attract much wildlife. A buzzard took a great interest in me on my scooter and swooped up and over several times.

FURTHER INFORMATION
Access Officer: 01387 260145

FACT FILE	
Map	Ordnance Survey Landranger Sheet 84
Start and Finish	Glenkiln (NX 837788)
Parking	Reservoir P
Toilets	Galloway Arms, Crocketford W/C
Distance	6 miles / 9.5 km circular
Landscape	Water / wood / hills / sculptures

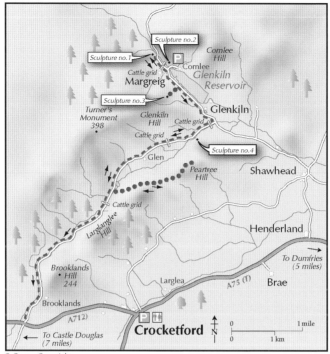

Rodin sculpture in Glenkiln

I came across the Langholm Initiative by accident when I was researching for another walk. Its members have researched, mapped and waymarked many walks, some more accessible than others, around Langholm. An excellent little book, *Langholm Walks,* describes twelve of these walks. I was very fortunate in having one of its members to guide me on their All Ability trail.

This trail is signposted as walk number 7, Jenny Noble's Gill, and starts at Kilngreen car park (north Langholm). Walk towards the town centre and turn right over the road bridge across the River Esk. Take the first left (Elizabeth Street) and go right at the end. Turn left into Buccleuch Park, where there is a chicane, which I just managed on my large countryside scooter. Follow the path through the park and take the left riverside route up a well-maintained, but fairly steep (1:9) track for another mile. The path then joins a farm track which takes you back to the A7. Unfortunately, at this point it becomes quite hazardous as the pavement over the bridge has no dropped kerb, and I was forced on to the road. However, as there are traffic lights at the bridge, I was at least in single lane traffic. After 200 to 300 yards there is the opportunity to rejoin the River Esk path, returning on the east of the river to the beginning.

Langholm is a beautiful place known as the Muckle Toon due to its history as a market town and centre of textiles and agriculture. Today there are only two textile firms which continue to provide much of the town's employment. It lies at the confluence of the River Esk and the Ewes Water. This walk offers an excellent variety of birdlife, some fine areas of woodland, and beautiful wildflowers in spring and summer.

FURTHER INFORMATION

Langholm Walks: 01387 380914 walks@langholm.initiative.co.uk

FACT FILE

Map	Ordnance Survey Landranger Sheet 79
Start and Finish	Kilngreen car park (NT 364849)
Parking	A7 P north & middle of Langholm
Toilets	A7 P north W/C (R) radar; A7 P middle W/C (R)
Distance	3 miles / 5 km circular
Landscape	Water / wood / town

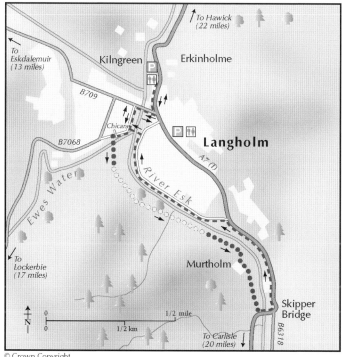

All Ability path, Langholm

50 Meggat Water

Dumfries & Galloway

When I was trying to decide which walks to include in this book I enquired, through an advert in disabled magazines, if anybody wished to suggest one. It is fitting, therefore, that the final walk, Meggat Water, was one suggested by a fellow wheelchair countryside enthusiast, who lives at the Samye Ling monastery in Eskdalemuir. And to my mind it is one of the best.

If you are seeking to be at peace with nature and to ramble along an easy trail going well up and into a river valley amidst the rolling hills of the Borders, then this is a good place to start. There is a car park for six cars at Bentpath but this adds 3 miles to the trail. As we wished to do at least 8 miles but still leave sufficient battery power to explore further, we parked at the side of the narrow tarmac road near Westkirk Mains. For the first 4 miles you are on the access road to four or five houses, only three of which appeared to be occupied and during four hours we were passed by just one tractor and one car. There are two cattle grids, one a mile up and then one a mile further on, but there are side gates which are easily opened. At the end of the tarmac road there is a fine piece of interpretation describing Glendinning, birthplace of Thomas Telford, the famous engineer. We continued up what was now a rough track for a mile and I could have kept going and going, well into the more remote countryside, had time and weather not dictated our return.

I am not a 'twitcher' but I do love watching birds and with our guide from the Langholm Initiative we identified a variety of birds. We saw two large buzzards, a flock of fieldfare, identifiable by their flight pattern, swallows, house martins and many small river birds.

I end this book with a feeling of real excitement for I know I will return to the Borders to explore their wonderful valleys.

FURTHER INFORMATION

Langholm Walks: 01387 380914 walks@langholm.initiative.co.uk

FACT FILE	
Map	Ordnance Survey Landranger Sheet 79
Start and Finish	Meggat Water (NT 296916 / NT 301984)
Parking	1.5 miles / 2.25 km northwest of Bentpath
Toilets	Langholm: A7 P north W/C (R) radar; A7 P middle W/C (R) attendant
Distance	5 miles / 8 km (10 miles / 16 km return)
Landscape	Rolling valley with a river

132

WALKING ON WHEELS

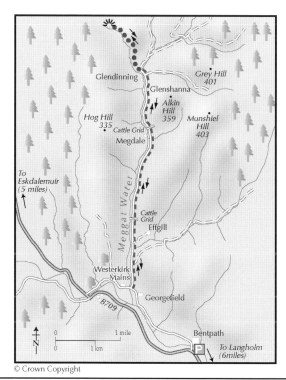

Road along Meggat Water

Useful Information

Travelling by Train

First ScotRail Disabled People's Protection Policy includes information on the facilities available at all stations in Scotland for people with disabilities.

* Download from: www.firstgroup.com/scotrail/content/pdfs/DPPP.pdf or request from: First ScotRail Customer Relations on 0845 601 5929 or email: scotrailcustomer.relations@firstgroup.com
* Before travelling, customers with special needs should contact: First ScotRail Helpline: Tel 0845 605 7021. Textphone 0845 602 0346
* For train operator and timetable information contact: National Rail Enquiry Service (NRES) 08457 48 49 50
* To plan a journey contact: Traveline Scotland 0870 608 2 608

Sustrans

Sustrans is the UK's leading sustainable transport charity and works on practical projects to encourage people to travel in ways that benefit their health and the environment. The charity is behind many groundbreaking projects including the National Cycle Network. The first 10,000 miles of safe and attractive cycling and walking routes have been completed bringing the Network to within 1 mile of 50% of the population.

For more information, visit the 'Access for Disabled People in Scotland' pages on: www.nationalcyclenetwork.org.uk, or telephone Sustrans in Edinburgh: 0131 539 8122

British Waterways

Venture on to any canal towpath in Scotland and you will soon see how the country's inland waterways have changed over the past few years.

From the newly restored Lowland canals to the magnificent Caledonian in the Highlands and the Crinan in Argyll, Scotland's canals are coming to life once again. With a wealth of wildlife and breathtaking scenery at every turn, Scotland's 200-year old network of canals is the perfect place to unwind and take time out from the hustle and bustle of everyday living.

Access to the country's waterways has always been a priority for British Waterways and over the past few years a host of improvements, including widened towpaths, disabled parking and other facilities, has ensured that more and more visitors can experience the many delights of the canal network.

As a result of the huge revitalisation effort in the Lowlands, visitors can now experience a mix of fantastic urban and rural settings as they journey from coast to coast along the Forth & Clyde Canal. And for those looking for a real 'Wow' then the spectacular Falkirk Wheel will not disappoint. The world's first and only rotating boat lift is an engineering marvel which is now firmly established as one of the country's leading tourist attractions and a true icon for Scotland.

For information visit: www.britishwaterways.co.uk or www.waterscape.com

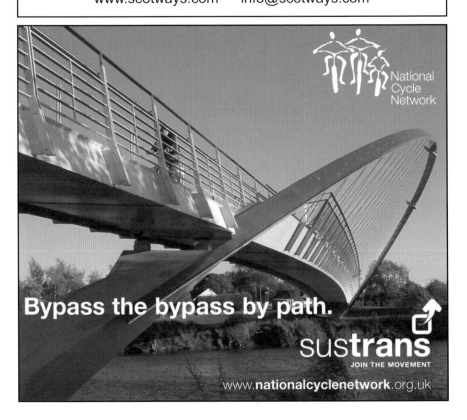

Multiple Sclerosis Society
Scotland

SCOTLAND HAS THE HIGHEST PREVALENCE OF MS IN THE WORLD

Multiple Sclerosis is the most common, potentially disabling neurological condition affecting young adults, with diagnosis typically around the age of 30

Please help – donations welcome

MULTIPLE SCLEROSIS SOCIETY SCOTLAND

Ratho Park, 88 Glasgow Road, Ratho Station, Newbridge EH28 8PP
Tel: 0131 335 4050 Fax: 0131 335 4051
E-mail: enquiries@mssocietyscotland.org.uk
www.mssocietyscotland.org.uk

Enabling everyone affected by multiple sclerosis to live life to their full potential until we find a cure

MS Society Scotland has over 35 Branches across Scotland, providing care and support for over 10,400 people with MS and thousands of others within the family network. Funding for all of the Society's services is achieved entirely by voluntary contributions.
Charity Reg: SCO 16433

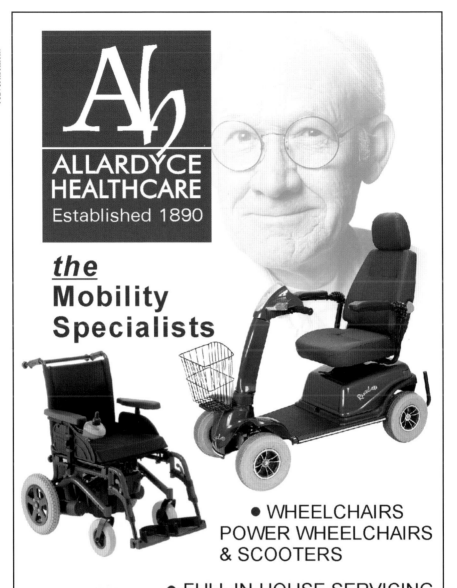

Art Gems
by Stella Morris

For paintings and commissions of your
favourite place please contact
stella@j-smorris.freeserve.co.uk
or telephone Stella on
0777 975 6401
for a friendly discussion under no obligation

Disclaimer

While Eva McCracken has surveyed the trails described in this book by personal travel in her own electric wheelchair or scooter during the period 2000–2005 and has described the trails to the best of her knowledge, neither she as author, nor Cualann Press Ltd as publishers, make any representation as to the completeness and the detailed accuracy of the information or of any opinions contained in this book. No warranty, expressed or implied as to the completeness or accuracy of the information contained herein is given. It is possible that weather or other events outwith the control of the author or the publishers could alter the condition of the trails described herein and those using this guide book as an aid to their enjoyment of the Scottish countryside do so fully at their own risk. Furthermore, advertisements do not imply endorsement of products or services by the author nor Cualann Press Ltd nor do they vouch for the accuracy of information provided in advertisements.

Excellent surface and superb scenery at Loch Katrine